ALABAMA TRAILS

Hiking & Backpacking North Alabama

By Richard Huey

Cover: Cheaha Mountain State Park

CONTENTS

INTRODUCTION

One thing that has always impressed me about the American Indian, whether in motion pictures or through literature, is their love for the land and the animals that inhabit it. Since moving to Alabama over 20 years ago, I have taken the time to enjoy the many lakes and forest lands. I have walked many trails the past several years in the southeastern states and discovered to my surprise there was no hiking guide to the trails of Alabama. While northern Georgia, North and South Carolina and a number of Tennessee guides are available to the outdoor enthusiast, Alabama lacked such a publication. I have therefore made this my goal the past year.

We have four National Forests in Alabama, two of which are covered in this guide, the Talladega and Bankhead National Forests.

Alabama has two designated wilderness areas, the Cheaha Wilderness in east central Alabama and the expanded Sipsey Wilderness in northwest Alabama. Alabama also has a great state park system with a number of parks offering excellent walking and hiking trails. Add a number of private and government trails, (county, municipal, TVA), and you will soon notice that Alabama has a lot to offer for anyone wanting to enjoy the outdoors.

Most of the trails in this publication are easy to moderate as far as a rating system being used. Some trails are more moderate to difficult. The physical condition of the individual hiker should be taken into consideration. What may be a moderate walk to some may be considered difficult to someone not in good physical condition. The distances mentioned throughout the book are estimated as close as possible to actual mileage except those areas where the State Parks or National Forest Service has established the distance between locations. In a number of instances, I have found trail signs and map distances to disagree (one such area is the Talladega National Forest, where one trail sign has 6 miles, another at the "opposite" trailhead has 8 miles and the map has 6.8 miles distance printed). A number of hiking clubs exist within north Alabama. I have listed some in the back of the book for those who wish to become more involved in hiking and backpacking. Outdoor stores have personnel who can help the beginning hiker and also have available a number of publications on hiking and backpacking. So, visit an outdoor store, contact a hiking club and begin to enjoy the beauty of Alabama's parks and trails.One final note on trails not included in this guide.   I found, during my travels around the state, that the Boy Scout Trails seem to be systematically ruined due to private property and building projects. I have therefore not included Boy Scout Trails, except the Desoto Scout Trail that merges with the Lookout Mountain Trail, in this book.   For information on available Scout Trails, contact your local Boy Scout organization.

ACKNOWLEDGEMENTS

I would like to express my appreciation to a number of people who helped in the development of this publication through their time and effort or sharing of valuable information. I would like to thank my son Kevin who hiked a number of trails with me and shuttled me to various trailheads. I would also like to thank my many friends in the Appalachian Trail Club of Alabama and the Sierra Club for sharing the outdoor experience on a number of trails.

Thanks go to Kim Smith and Kent Davenport with the Talladega National Forest Service for their assistance and also to Allen Polk of the National Forest Office in Montgomery. There are a number of other forest service personnel who contributed valuable information.

I would like to thank Tim Haney and Talmadge Butler from Desoto State Park, Mike Storm from Lake Lurleen State Park and other state park personnel who were so helpful. I also wish to thank Carroll Wilson and Jim Austin from the Alabama Trails Association for valuable information furnished.

I wish to thank Linda Walker for her support and advice. I would especially like to thank Danny Crownover in Gadsden for his time and effort and indispensable help to help this project become a reality.

TIPS FOR THE BEGINNER

The first thing that I would like to mention for those just getting into hiking and backpacking is PHYSICAL CONDITIONING. One should consider walking the shorter trails that require less physical exertion and gradually hike the longer, more strenuous trails as they improve their own physical condition. While an experienced hiker may walk 2-3 miles per hour on level terrain, those who may be "out of shape" should walk at a slower more comfortable pace.

Since the hiker depends on his or her feet to get him to his destination, FOOTCARE is a very important factor to consider. While some easier trails can be walked while wearing tennis or similar low-cut style shoes, many trails are very rocky and include numerous ascending and descending steep grades. A high-top, hiking boot would be highly recommended for these trails. Ankle support and thick soles are two features of most good hiking boots. Socks that wick perspiration away from the skin are much better than cotton socks that absorb perspiration. Blisters caused from new shoes, wet socks or incorrect shoe size can make for a miserable experience. New shoes should be "broken in" prior to any long hike.

Proper CLOTHING is another factor that helps increase the enjoyment of the outing. Shorts and short sleeve shirts may be very comfortable during hot weather, while long pants and long sleeve shirts may be necessary on cool spring or autumn hikes. While bluejeans are typical attire at home, they are not the most comfortable pants for hiking. Instead, pants that are somewhat loose fitting are more comfortable for hiking up and down hills. On cold winter days, a hat and even gloves should be considered as optional clothing items.

FOOD and WATER can make the difference between an enjoyable outing or a very exhausting hike, particularly in very hot weather. Lack of adequate water supply or snack foods during long hikes or in hot weather can tire out a hiker very quickly.

One additional item that I would like to mention to the beginning hiker is the use of a hiking stick. While some hikers elect not to use a hiking stick, I have found one to be useful in several ways. Along with knocking down those spider webs sometimes found across the trail, your stick can also be used to help clear briars and tall weeds on the trail. I have also found my stick very useful when ascending or descending steep terrain and for balance when fording streams.

SAFETY

Lack of good judgment may be the most serious hazard to hikers and backpackers, especially beginners. Hiking alone is not recommended by most outdoor specialists; however. for those who travel alone, a written itinerary, including destination and approximate time of return, should be left with a friend or relative.

Weather conditions should always be taken into consideration for any hiking trip. Know what the weather forecast is for the area you may be visiting and take the proper clothing, such as rain gear.

Most "outdoor" literature will have a list of "essential" items recommended to take on hiking trips. These usually include appropriate maps, compass, whistle, matches (in a watertight container), flashlight, a first aid kit and perhaps rain gear. Experience will usually show these items to be worth carrying. Food and adequate water supply (2-4 quarts per day) are very important to any hiker. Whenever obtaining water on the trail, it should be treated by one of the three methods recommended by outdoor specialists. The most effective method is to boil before use. A second method is to use a water filter device, available at most outdoor stores, The third and easiest method is to use purification tablets, also available at outdoor stores.

Hunting is allowed on national forest lands in accordance with state laws. Primitive camping is restricted by district rangers to those with written permission. Hikers should stay on the trail during hunting season and wear bright clothing.

One very important danger for anyone just getting into hiking and backpacking is HYPOTHERMIA. Hypothermia is the subnormal temperature of the body caused by exposure to cold and aggravated by wind, rain and exhaustion. Symptoms include shivering, slurred speech, impaired judgment, weakness and loss of coordination. A final symptom is unconsciousness. Treatment for someone suffering from hypothermia should include: getting the victim out of wind and rain, changing them into dry clothing and, if necessary into a warm sleeping bag, administering warm drinks and seeing that they rest. Many people do not realize that the temperature does not have to be freezing for hypothermia to occur.

One last danger is poisonous snakes. The very thought of snakes inhibits some people from enjoying our great outdoors. Alabama is home to the copperhead, cottonmouth and coral snake. However, in several years of hiking across the state, I have only encountered one poisonous snake. That was off the trail. Hikers should stay on the trail and watch where they sit when resting. The fact that snakes are normally nocturnal should calm some fears.

NATIONAL FOREST TRAILS

Alabama has four national forests containing over 640,000 acres. They are managed by a forest supervisor and several district rangers. Information can be obtained by writing to the state office in Montgomery or any of the district offices listed in the back of this publication. Two of the forests are covered in this book.

Within the Talladega National Forest lies the Cheaha Wilderness and within the Bankhead National Forest lies the expanded Sipsey Wilderness. Both of these areas offer great hiking and backpacking.

An abundance of wildlife can be found in the forests, including deer, wild turkey. waterfowl, a number of owls and hawks, squirrel, quail, woodpecker and a variety of turtles. The Alabama Department of Conservation and Natural Resources operates six wildlife management areas within the national forests.

Recreational activities available to visitors include picnicking, camping, hiking, swimming, hunting,fishing and boating. Horse trails are also available on both the Talladega and Bankhead as well as ORV (off road vehicles) trails.

TALLADEGA NATIONAL FOREST

The Talladega National Forest is located in east central Alabama. It's 217,000 acres encompass the southernmost thrust of the Appalachian Mountain chain. Cheaha Mountain, the highest point in the state, and Cheaha State Park are included within the forest boundaries. Long ridges, rock cliffs and wooded valleys are part of the outdoor experience within the Talladega Forest.

Located midway between Birmingham and Atlanta, the forest is easily accessible and offers over 85 camping and picnic areas. Several lakes offer swimming and fishing. Cheaha State Park, located near the middle of the national forest and on top of 2,407' Cheaha Mountain, offers motel rooms, cabins, a group lodge plus camping facilities.

The Pinhoti Trail, designated in 1977 as a National Recreation Trail, stretches over 80 miles from north of Sylacauga to near Piedmont and is presently being extended to near the Georgia state line. Several connecting trails near Cheaha make that area a great place to hike or backpack.

Wildlife within the forest include deer, turkey, rabbit, squirrel, opossum, bobcat, raccoon, quail, waterfowl and a number of owls and hawks. Plant life includes muscadines, blueberries, wild cherries, wild strawberries and persimmons.

Talladega National Forest

PINHOTI TRAIL

This is Alabama's longest hiking trail, stretching over 80 miles through the Talladega National Forest in east central Alabama. It was designated as a National Recreation Trail in 1977 and is still being extended, to eventually reach from near Sylacauga to Piedmont and the Georgia state line.

The trail "travels" through a variety of terrain, through hard-wood forests, along small streams, through hollows, below rock bluffs and along mountain ridges. The northern sections of the trail include terrain with gentle grades with few steep grades that cover short distances. The southern area around Horseblock Mountain and Cheaha State Park is more rugged, with steep terrain covering longer distances. Hikers should wear sturdy shoes when hiking this area.

A variety of plant life awaits the hiker along the Pinhoti, including blueberries, muscadines,wild cherries and wild strawber-ries. Animal life includes deer, wild turkey, raccoons, squirrel, beaver and a variety of birds, including owls and hawks.

I have divided the Pinhoti into 10 sections due to its length. Each section may be hiked individually in either direction as a day hike or combined with other sections as a backpacking trip. Some sections, especially around Cheaha Mountain, are long enough to provide good backpacking trips.

Presently, there are only 3 trail shelters along the entire trail, but plans are being made for future construction of others as funds permit. There are numerous sites however, for camping along the trail. I have notated many of these. I strongly urge hikers to use "no-trace" camping procedures in order to leave the forest as they found it. This way, other hikers will also be able to enjoy the area in its natural state.

Camping permits are needed from the District Ranger offices during hunting season.

Water sources are not available on some sections of the trail, so be sure to take plenty of water with you. Any water that is obtained along the trail should be treated, either by boiling, use of a filtering device, or chemical tablets.

The present Pinhoti trail map is not very good by itself. A Talladega National Forest map will help; but I recommend the use of topographic maps for some sections. A new and better trail map is being developed, but is not yet available.

SECTION 1 (8.5 Miles) *Moderate*
CR 55 to FR 500 (Coleman Lake)

This is the northernmost section of the trail that has been completed and marked. However, there are no trailhead signs with distances to locations. The Alabama Trails Association, National Forest Service and other groups have obtained land north of CR 55 and are in the process of expanding the Pinhoti Trail, hopefully to the Georgia state line.

From the trail sign on CR 55, walk S through thick overgrowth before crossing an old forest road at approximately .5 mile. Continue walking S for a short distance before reaching Choccolocco Lake. The trail will head SW along the ridge as it parallels the lake. Cross the earthen dam at approximately 1.0 mile. The trail will continue SE along the ridge, reaching the south end of the lake at approximately 1.5 miles.

The trail will continue along this ridge for the next 1.5 miles, gradually swinging to the south. At approximately 2.9 miles, the trail will turn E and cross a saddle. The next .6 mile will wind along a narrow trail around the ridge. At approximately 3.5 miles, the trail will descend moderately to steep, as it makes its way between two ridges. The trail will then bear right and descend, with a creek on your left. At 4.0 miles, the trail will turn SE and parallel Choccolocco Creek on your left. At 4.5 miles, the trail will cross the creek and pick up again on the opposite side.

This crossing can be confusing, since there are no markers to rely on. The hiker will have to wade the stream and head SE to pick up the trail parallel to the stream.

Cross a small creek at approximately 4.8 miles. The trail will continue on an old roadbed and pass through thick overgrowth. The trail picks up Choccolocco Creek again at approximately 5.5 miles and continues S, parallel to the creek. Cross Choccolocco Creek and a smaller creek before heading SE with the creek on your left. At 6.0 miles, cross Choccolocco Creek again. The trail will parallel the creek before crossing a third time at approximately 6.2 miles. After crossing another small creek, the trail makes its way through an area dominated by many ferns and hardwood trees. Hike along a ridge with a small creek on your left. Gradually ascend and continue hiking SE before reaching FR 540 at approximately 7.0 miles.

The trail will make its way along a ridge, heading E and then S. Cross a horse trail at approximately 7.5 miles and bear left. Cross a firebreak at approximately 7.8 miles and another firebreak at 8.2 miles. Reach FR 500 50 yards E of the Coleman Lake parking area.

The trail sign for the Pinhoti Trail on CR 55 can be reached by driving N on Ala. Hwy 9 west of Heflin for 12 miles from its junction with U.S. Hwy 78. Turn right at the blinking traffic light onto CR 262. Drive 4.5 miles and park on the side of the road. (a parking area is planned for the future) CR 55 merges with CR 262 shortly after you turn off of Hwy 9.

The Coleman Lake parking area and trailhead can be reached by turning N onto FR 500 just west of Heflin, where the sign for the Talladega Forest Work Center and Talladega Scenic Drive is located. Continue N on FR 500 for 8 miles to Pine Glen Campground and another 5 miles to the Coleman Lake parking area. FR 500 also intersects CR 55 north of Coleman Lake and east of the trailhead on CR 55. A Talladega National Forest map will help to locate these roads.

SECTION 2 (6.8 Miles) *Easy*
FR 500 (Coleman Lake) to FR 500 (Pine Glen Campground)

This section of the Pinhoti is popular because it has a shelter along the trail as well as developed campgrounds at both ends. Sweetwater Lake is also a good camping site between Laurel Shelter and Pine Glen Campground.

The northern trailhead for this section is actually located on FR 500 west of the Coleman Lake Campground and Lake. From the small parking area, the trail leads S and passes west of Coleman Lake at approximately 1.0 mile. Continue walking south and cross

Pinhoti Trail - View of Cheaha Mountain

FR 553D. Reach Shoal Creek Church at approximately 1.6 miles. This hand-hewn log church was built between 1885 and 1890 and is listed in the National Register of Historic Places. A small cemetery with graves of early settlers lies closeby.

From the church, the trail swings westward and crosses FR 553 at approximately 2.0 miles. The trail soon turns southward and reaches Laurel Shelter at 3.2 miles. This is one of only two trail shelters on the northern half of the Pinhoti. A third shelter is located south of Cheaha State Park. The National Forest Service plans on constructing more trail shelters whenever funds permit.

From the shelter, the trail continues southward and passes by the western side of Sweetwater Lake, an 86 acre man-made reservoir, at approximately 4.3 miles. A good campsite area is located on the southern part of the lake. The trail continues past the earthen dam on the south end of the lake and heads westward, crossing a field. After crossing the field, the trail will parallel Shoal Creek for approximately two miles as it flows southward. Reach FR 500 and Pine Glen Campground area at approximately 6.8 miles (the sign at Coleman Lake parking area lists this section as 8.0 miles distance while the sign at Pine Glen Campground lists the distance as 6.0 miles. The actual distance is close to the trail map's 6.8 miles).

Coleman Lake trailhead and Pine Glen Campground can be reached by driving north on FR 500 located west of Heflin. Turn at the sign for the Talladega National Forest work center and Talladega Scenic Drive.

SECTION 3 (13 Miles) *Moderate*
FR 500 (Pine Glen Campground) to U.S. Hwy 78

This section of the Pinhoti Trail runs from Pine Glen Campground on FR 500 to the Talladega National Forest work center near U.S. Hwy 78 west of Heflin.

The trail starts just south of the campground entrance and heads SW, with the campground on your right. You will soon cross a forest road and a small creek. Ascend. At approximately 1.0 mile, the trail will swing NW and then SE as it follows the ridge. Good views of Shoal Creek can be seen on your right. Descend SW with a forest road on your left and Shoal Creek on your right. Reach a forest road at approximately 1.3 miles. Walk to your right 50 yards on the road. The trail will continue on your left, heading E, then S. The trail soon bears SE along a ridge, with Highrock Lake on your right. You will soon bear left (E), cross a small creek and ascend. Cross FR 531 at approximately 1.6 miles. Cross a small creek and ascend. Continue S along the side of a ridge. Descend and reach a stream at approximately 2.3 miles.

Cross the stream and pick up the trail again to the right of the small rock dam, heading W. The trail will swing S along the side of a ridge with the stream on your right. Cross a small creek and bear W through a "low lying area" with the stream still on your right. After the trail becomes wider, you will be heading S. Cross a small creek and ascend at approximately 3.0 miles. You will soon pass a large area on your right (downhill) suitable for camping. Continue S along the west side of a ridge. Cross an old forest road above the creek and descend. The trail continues W along the creek before crossing at approximately 3.5 miles (a suitable campsite). Ascend. Continue S, as the trail follows the ridge, and cross a forest road, that will parallel the trail for a short distance. Continue S along the east side of the ridge and cross the forest road again at approximately 4.2 miles. The trail continues S. then W, then S again before descending on an old forest road. Continue descending along the hillside and reach two creeks that merge at 5.0 miles.

Walk to your right (W) and cross the creek. The Lower Shoal Shelter will be on your left, next to the stream. The trail continues southward, gradually ascending. Make several switchbacks before crossing an old forest road at approximately 5.3 miles. Follow the ridgeline, crossing FR 531 at 6.0 miles. The trail will continue to follow the ridge for the next two miles, as it heads southward. Reach an area at approximately 8.3 miles with good views to the west. The trail soon makes two switchbacks, swings around the ridge and descends.

Cross FR 523 at 9.0 miles. Ascend and head SE. Nice views to the SW can soon be seen before the trail descends and swings around another ridge. Descend along the ridge. At 10.0 miles, the trail will swing around another ridge with good views to the west. Pass through a "cut" area of forest as the trail makes several switchbacks. Ascend along the ridge and reach a rocky outcrop area with a small campsite nearby at approximately 11.0 miles. The trail will make two switchbacks as it continues to follow the ridgeline. Ascend and swing around the ridge at approximately 11.4 miles. Good views of Choccolocco Mountain to the W can be seen before reaching another rocky outcrop area. The trail then makes several switchbacks before heading W along the ridge at approximately 11.8 miles.

Descend, cross a watershed and ascend. FR 500 will soon be on your left. At 12.2 miles, the trail heads W and follows the ridge before descending. Cross FR 500 and continue S. Pass through a small pine growth area, descend and cross a small creek. Reach the trailhead sign at 13.0 miles. FR 500 on your right leads 8.0 miles to the Pine Glen Campground. The Pinhoti Trail continues southward after crossing the railroad tracks and walking across the bridge over U.S. Hwy 78.

There is available parking at the Pine Glen Campground area and near the Talladega National Forest work center just off U.S. Hwy 78.

SECTION 4 (4.4 Miles) *Easy*
U.S. Hwy 78 to Ala. Hwy 281

This section, like section 5, is short enough for a day hike and may be included in a weekend backpacking trip. The trail is easy to walk and can be hiked in 2.5 to 3 hours. The trail picks up at the south end of the bridge over U.S. Hwy 78 at the northern terminus of the Talladega Scenic Drive. From the bridge, the trail heads W along the side of a hill with U.S. Hwy 78 on your right. Pass under power lines and cross a forest road. The trail will parallel the highway for a short distance at approximately .4 mile. Descend along the ridge and cross an old forest road. The trail will make several switchbacks as it descends. Cross a small creek and continue W. Cross another forest road and ascend (S) from the ridge at approximately .9 mile. The trail will turn W along a ridge before descending and becoming narrow. Reach a clearing with good views to the W. The trail will continue across the clearing and descend. Reach another ridge at approximately 1.4 miles.

The trail will descend steeply via switchbacks. Cross over a ridge and descend SE along the ridge. Bear right (W), cross a creek with unique rock formations and ascend along the ridge at approximately 2.0 miles. Continue S along the ridge before bearing to your right (W) around the ridge. The trail will head SE and reach Ala. Hwy 281 at approximately 2.4 miles. Cross the highway and descend. Walk SW before turning E around the ridge. The trail turns S before crossing a forest road. Gradually descend and cross another forest road at 3.0 miles. The trail winds its way E, then S. Cross a fire break and descend at approximately 3.4 miles.

Cross a creek and ascend. Switchbacks to the NW and S around the ridge precede another descent. Cross another creek and ascend. The trail then swings around a ridge and reaches a creek on your right with a good camp site, At 4.0 miles, cross an "open area." The trail then turns W and N before swinging around to the SW. Reach the north end of the bridge over 1-20 at 4.4 miles

Ala. Hwy 281 leads north to its terminus with U.S. Hwy 78 and south to Cheaha State Park. Section 5 of the Pinhoti Trail continues south of the bridge.

SECTION 5 (4.2 Miles) *Easy/Moderate*
Ala. Hwy 281 to U.S. Hwy 431

This section of the trail can be walked by itself or with section 4 to make an 8.6 mile hike. The terrain is easy to moderate and can be walked in 4.5 to 5 hours.

From the southern end of the bridge over 1-20, the trail will head S. Cross over a ridge and descend via switchbacks. At .2 mile, cross a small creek and ascend. Bear right (W) before crossing a logging road. At .6 mile, cross a forest road near its junction with a gravel road. Descend SW before crossing a watershed. The trail then heads N and swings around the ridge heading SW again. Bear left and cross an old forest road. Descend and cross a creek at 1.2 miles.

Ascend and cross over the ridge via switchbacks. Continue W and descend. Hike N before crossing a creek via a footbridge at 1.6 miles (a suitable campsite). Ascend. Continue W along a ridge and cross an old forest road. The trail will continue to head W, then S. Reach FR 518 at 2.2 miles. Pick up the trail again 30' to your right. After crossing the road, the trail will make a semi-circle around the ridge. Descend from the ridge at approximately 2.7 miles. Reach a small creek at approximately 3.2 miles. Hike along the creek, then W through a hollow and S along a ridge for a short distance. Descend SW from the ridge at approximately 3.8 miles.

Reach a trailhead sign and U.S. Hwy 431 at 4.2 miles. The trail will continue across the highway and 50 yards north. The gravel road leads to the next trailhead.

Ala. Hwy 281 is also known as the Talladega Scenic Drive. It connects U.S. Hwy 78 just west of Heflin with Cheaha State park and runs along the crest of Talladega Mountain. The drive is particularly beautiful in the fall with a number of overlooks providing panoramic views of the Talladega National Forest area.

SECTION 6 (5.3 Miles) *Moderate*
U.S. Hwy 431 to CR 24

The length of this section, like several others, enables one to day hike or backpack when hiked along with the next one or two sections of the trail.

The trail continues approximately 50 yards N on Hwy 431 where the gravel road on the west intersects the highway. Walk up the road for 250 yards before reaching a parking area and trailhead sign.

The trail heads SW, reaching a "thick brush" area at .2 mile. Descend and cross a creek at .4 mile. The trail will head S with the creek on your right. The trail will then turn E before crossing a creek and turning back to the S. Cross a smaller creek at .7 mile, where it merges with a larger creek. Cross the larger creek four times before reaching a suitable campsite at .9 mile. The trail will ascend and become narrow along the ridge. Continue S and cross a forest road at approximately 1.2 miles. At 1.6 miles, the trail will descend SW.

When the trail turns to the W, you will come to another suitable camping area. Cross several watersheds at approximately 2.2 miles as the trail heads S. Descend and hike W, then S before crossing two small creeks. The trail will then head SW and wind around a ridge. Cross a creek four times before ascending. I found this area of the Pinhoti to be a very nice hike, especially in the Fall. Continue S, cross the creek and ascend before making a switchback to your right. You will hear a small waterfall on your right as the trail winds N around the ridge at approximately 2.8 miles.

The trail will turn to the W before descending on your right. Cross a creek at approximately 3.2 miles and hike S along the creek. Cross the creek again and ascend. Continue S along the creek before crossing a smaller creek. Hike NW along the hill and cross a forest road at 3.7 miles. The trail will turn W, cross another forest road and head N. After a short distance, the trail will turn W and intersect a forest road on top of the ridge at approximately 4.0 miles. Walk along this road for 60 yards.

The trail will descend on your left (S) down a ridge to a creek. Cross the creek twice by way of rocks and a short distance further, an old log. Continue SW with the creek on your left. Morgan Lake will soon be on your left. Cross an old forest road at approximately 4.6 miles. Descend SW and bear right near the bottom of the ridge (a well worn path will wind around the base of the ridge to Morgan Lake). The Pinhoti will descend on your right before crossing a small creek. After crossing the creek, the trail swings S for 75 yards before intersecting CR 24 at 5.2 miles. The trail will continue across the road.

SECTION 7 (12.2 Miles) *Moderate/Strenuous*
CR 24 to Cheaha State Park,

I found this section of the Pinhoti to be both tranquil and scenic with good available water between CR 24 and Blue Mountain and great views from the Blue Mountain area. There are a number of good camping areas south of CR 24.

From CR 24, the trail ascends to the nearby ridge where you bear to your left along the ridge. At approximately .4 mile, descend and cross an old trail. Here you will bear S along the ridge, descend and cross a small creek. The trail will bear left and ascend to the next ridge (There were small camping sites along the creek). Reach the crest of the ridge at approximately .8 mile. Continue SW (the old trail will continue NE) for 75 yards, then bear left (S).

At approximately 1.0 mile, the trail will head SE between two small ridges. Ascend along the ridge, heading SW, with a small creek below on your left. At 1.4 miles, ascend SE and walk along the ridge. The trail will bear right at 1.5 miles and ascend NW (an old trail descends between the ridges). Look for the trail markings on the trees. Pass through a saddle and ascend to the ridge. Descend, cross another saddle and ascend again. Continue along the ridge.

At approximately 2.0 miles, descend. The trail will split in two directions. Bear left (SW). Look for two marked trees (the old trail to the right will lead north). You will soon cross an unnamed creek and continue parallel to the creek. This area is a good camp site with plenty of water available. At approximately 3.0 miles, cross another small creek, which flows into the larger creek.

The trail will turn to your left where a 3rd small creek merges with the larger creek and head in a southward direction. You will cross this small creek 3 times as you gradually ascend between two ridges. There is a small camp site where you cross the creek for the 3rd time. Here the trail will turn S while the creek continues east. Ascend by way of a switchback to your right, as the trail now heads W again. Cross an old road on the ridge. A switchback to your right leads N, as you descend and then SW by way of a second switchback between two ridges.

Reach Hillabee Creek at approximately 4.0 miles. This is a good site for camping, with plenty of water. Cross the large creek by way of rocks. You will soon cross under power lines through heavy brush and ascend by way of a switchback on an old forest road. The trail will make an immediate switchback to your left (S) off the road (look for marked trees). Ascend and bear right (W) before descending. Ascend (SW) again to a saddle. Bear right (W) and ascend. Continue along the ridge. Reach a "cut area" at approximately 4.5 miles with thick growth. Continue W and pass by the remains of an old van. Descend to a small creek at approximately 4.8 miles. Bear right (N) along the base of the ridge and cross a creek with good camp sites at 5.0 miles.

The trail will follow the edge of the ridge (trail is very narrow), then between two ridges with a small creek on your right. Cross a "flat lowland area" at approximately 5.4 miles, then continue along the ridge on your left, heading S. Cross a watershed and bear left along the base of the ridge with a creek on your right. Cross the creek and bear left (SW). Ascend along the ridge. The trail will swing around the ridge (NW to S), then ascend at approximately 6.0 miles.

Continue SW between two ridges and ascend, gradually heading S. Reach an old grass covered roadbed and continue S. Cross FR 589 at 7.0 miles. A sign lists the distances back to CR 24 and Cheaha State Park.

The trail will make a switchback to your right, heading NW. A series of switchbacks will ascend and wander around the ridges as the trail makes its way up Blue Mountain. At 8.0 miles, the trail ascends steeply for a short distance, then gradually before reaching the top of the ridge. Continue S along the ridge (the trail was not well marked when I hiked this area due to a number of downed trees from storm damage). Pass by rock formations on the ridge top at approximately 9.0 miles. Ascend gradually along the ridge. Reach a rocky crest with large rock formations at 9.5 miles. At approximately 10 miles, reach a signpost listing Blue Mountain as 1.0 mile (the Blue Mt. Trail ascends for .5 mile to Bald Rock overlook in Cheaha State Park)

Continue S, descending. Reach a rocky area, where again the trail was not well marked as other sections. Make a switch back to your left at a "marked" tree, then descend to your right (look for markings on rocks as well as trees). The trail will bear R heading west before crossing a watershed and ascending to the S and E. Cross another rocky area before ascending S (a small camp site will be on the left of the trail) and passing through an overgrown area. At approximately 11 miles, cross another rocky area and ascend steeply before the trail levels out. Good views to the N and E can be had before the trail descends (E, then SW). Ascend SW, then W as the trail makes its way around the ridge. Cross a watershed and rocky area and ascend. Hike SW along the side of the ridge, cross a watershed and bear Left (S). Ascend gradually along the ridge at approximate 12 miles. Reach the paved Ala. highway 281 at 12.2 miles. This road leads .2 mile to the Cheaha State Park entrance and .3 mile left to the parking area for the Cave Creek Trail and Odum Scout Trailheads.

SECTION 8 (12 Miles) *Moderate/Strenous*
Cheaha State Park to Adams Gap

This section of the Pinhoti is the most heavily traveled, due to its location atop Cheaha Mountain. A number of overlooks provide great views of the mountain and surrounding forest. Several trails intersect atop the mountain at Caney Head Shelter, the only shelter on the southern part of the Pinhoti Trail. Cheaha State Park and nearby Lake Chinnabee provide developed campsites, from which day hikes can be taken on the Pinhoti and other nearby trails.

This section of the Pinhoti begins on Ala. highway 281, between the park entrance and the parking area where the road curves sharply before entering the park. You soon arrive at a trail junction. The Odum Scout Trail will bear left and end near the parking area on 281. The trailhead for the Cave Creek trail is located a short distance ahead. The Pinhoti Trail will continue on your right. (A trail sign lists the distances for Caney Head Shelter and Adams Gap)

At approximately .8 mile, cross an old jeep road. There is a good campsite just ahead and great views of Cheaha Lake and the Talladega Forest below. Continue along the ridge and begin ascending for a short distance. At approximately 1.4 miles, the trail makes its way through and over large rocks to the ridge top at Hernandes Peak. There is a small campsite here.

At approximately 1.9 miles, you will come to the Cheaha Wilderness boundary, marked by a dedication plaque in the rock. A short distance ahead, you will come to a trail sign listing distances back to Cheaha State Park (2.0 miles) and ahead to the shelter (4 miles). The trail will descend for a while via switchbacks before leveling out at approximately 2.3 miles. This is another area suitable for camping. At 2.5 miles, ascend and reach a rocky area with excellent views of the Talladega Forest below and Cheaha State Park

16.

to the north.

Reach a junction at approximately 2.9 miles, with a spur trail leading 1/4 mile to McDill Point. This is a very good overlook with excellent views of Talladega Mountain to the south and the Talladega Forest area below. The Pinhoti Trail will swing around the ridge, heading east, then north as it ascends and descends several times. Another camping area is located where the trail again turns to the east. The trail soon turns southward and gradually ascends.

Reach a Cheaha Wilderness sign at approximately 3.8 miles. Cross a rocky area and reach another trail junction at 4.0 mile. The Cave Creek and Nubbin Creek trails can be reached by ascending up the ridge (the Cave Creek Trail leads back to Cheaha State Park via the east side of the mountain while the Nubbin Creek Trail descends to Nubbin Creek road on the east side of the mountain and intersects with the Odum Scout Trail south of Caney Head Shelter). The Pinhoti Trail continues to the right. A sign lists Caney Head Shelter as 2 miles ahead. The remainder of the trail to the shelter will run along the top of the mountain.

At approximately 5.0 miles, a rocky cliff area affords great views of McDill Point on your right, Talladega Mountain to your left and the forest below. Reach Caney Head Shelter at 6.0 miles. Here, the Odum Scout Trail and the Chinnabee Silent Trail intersect the Pinhoti Trail. The Odum Scout Trail leads 4.7 miles down Cedar Mountain, past High Falls, to a trailhead just off FR 650 near Pyriton. The Chinnabee Silent Trail descends and makes its way 6.0 miles to its terminus at Chinnabee Lake. A fairly reliable water source is located just a few yards down the Chinnabee Silent Trail on your left (during summer months, you may want to check with forest personnel or Cheaha State Park personnel as to the water availability). The shelter and nearby area are heavily used by groups of hikers. Smaller campsites are available just a short distance south.

From the shelter and trail junction, the Pinhoti continues SW along the west side of the mountain. Reach a campsite area at approximately 6.6 miles, with a rocky cliff affording very good views of the forest below. Ascend to another overlook before continuing along the ridge. At 7.2 miles, come to a thick overgrowth area. A steep ascent leads to a rocky overlook with great views of the mountain and surrounding forest.

The trail will descend, via switchbacks, through a large boulder area at approximately 7.5 miles. This area has been recently re-marked and is much easier to follow than when I first hiked the trail. This area is the hardest part of the trail if backpacking, due to walking over the large rocks and descending as steeply as it does. After passing through the large boulders, the trail continues descend-ing gradually. Reach a sign and old forest road at approximately 8.5 miles. Turn right (NE) onto this road and follow it for approximately 400 yards. Here a sign directs the hiker SW while the road continues northward. The remainder of this section of the trail will wander along the base of the mountain, around several ridges, and crossing several very small creeks. At approximately 11 miles, you will see FR 600 on your right, as the trail parallels the road to Adams Gap. It is 6 miles to County Road 42 to the right and 6 miles to Clairmont Gap to your left via FR 600. The Pinhoti trail continues across the road as it makes its way for another 11 miles to its southern terminus at Chandler Springs.

SECTION 9 (6 Miles) *Moderate*
Adams Gap to Clairmont Gap

This section of the trail picks up on the west side of FR 600. From the road, descend and cross a watershed. The Skyway Loop Trail intersects the Pinhoti Trail approximately .1 mile from FR 600. This junction was not marked by any sign when I hiked the trails. (the Skyway Loop Trail leads 6 miles to intersect the Chinnabee Silent Trail near Lake Chinnabee)

The trail crosses over several very rocky areas within the first mile. At approximately 1.2 miles, you will make two switchbacks to your right after crossing 2 watershed areas. Descend and cross the first of two small creeks. Hike over a small hill and cross the second creek before ascending through another rocky area. After several switchbacks, reach an old road (637-R) at 1.8 miles.

Cross the road and begin ascending SE. Make a switchback to your R and continue W along the ridge. Good views of the Talladega can be seen during winter months. The trail will come close to FR

600 on your left and cross the road at approximately 3 miles. Reach rock formations to the left of the trail at approximately 3.6 miles. Here you can get good views to the SE and SW. At 4.0 miles, cross FR 600 again. The trail continues SW along the ridge. Reach the top of the ridge at approximately 4.7 miles and hike along the overgrown rocky terrain. Good views to the W & N can be had from this area. At 5.2 miles, begin descending. A rocky ledge provides excellent views of the mountain chain and the Talladega Forest. Switchbacks that lead back to your right, below the cliffs, and then left, will take you down to Clairmont Gap at 6.0 miles. The sign only notates locations to the north, since the next section of the trail leading south to Chandler Springs was completed only recently. From the Gap, FR 600 leads 6 miles back to Adams Gap and south 5 miles to Chandler Springs. County Road 103, which intersects FR 600, leads to Ala. Highway 77 and north to Munford.

SECTION 10 (5 Miles) *Moderate*
Clairmont Gap to Chandler Springs

This section, like section # 1, has been added since publication of the present Pinhoti Trail Map. An up-to-date trail map is being assembled by the Nation Forest Office in Montgomery, but no date has been set for its publication when I last talked to forest rangers.

From Clairmont Gap, the Pinhoti Trail continues on the west side of FR 600 after crossing the road junction. The trail continues its SW direction as it passes along the north side of the ridge over very rocky terrain. At approximately 1.0 mile, the trail becomes easier until you again cross over rocky terrain at 1.5 miles. At approximately 1.8 miles, the trail will veer right (NW) before swinging around the ridge and heading south. A small creek is located downhill on your right . You will ascend briefly before reaching FR 600 at approximately 2.0 miles.

After crossing FR 600, the trail will swing around to your right as it continues on the south side of the ridge. At 2.2 miles, a rocky overlook to the left of the trail offers very good views from east to west. At approximately 2.4 miles, the trail will bear left (E), then right (S) as it descends. Continue along the ridge before again descending.   At 2.9 miles, swing around to your right (N) along the side of the ridge.

At approximately 3.3 miles, switchback to your left (W) and descend gradually. Cross a small creek at 3.5 miles and ascend SW between two ridges. You will soon make a switchback to your left (E) before ascending south, then west along the ridge.

At 4.0 miles, cross FR 600 again and continue west between the road on your left and the ridge on your right. The trail will swing through a gap to the north side of the ridge and continue west. Reach a saddle at approximately 4.5 miles and ascend to the ridge.   Continue along the ridge.   At approximately 4.8 miles, you will begin descending and switchback to your right (N). A second switchback to your left runs through an overgrown area before reaching the road at approximately 5.0 miles. (the trail will cut back to the right for approximately 100 yards before reaching the trail sign and road)

It is 1/2 mile to your left to FR 600, and another 5 miles to Clairmont Gap via FR 600.

CHINNABEE SILENT TRAIL *Moderate/Strenous*

This trail is adequately named, since it was built from 1973-76 by the Boy Scout Troop 29 from the Alabama School For The Deaf in Talladega and connects Lake Chinnabee and the Pinhoti Trail on Talladega Mountain. The 6 mile trail begins near the southern end of Lake Chinnabee, which is located just west of Cheaha State Park.

From the trailhead sign, the trail follows Cheaha Creek. A trail sign for the Lakeshore Trail is posted 50 yards from the trailhead (this 2 mile trail follows the shoreline of Lake Chinnabee). Another 100 yards brings you to the trail sign for the Skyway Loop Trail. This 6 mile trail wanders through variable terrain before intersecting the Pinhoti Trail at Adams Gap on FS Road 600. The Chinnabee Silent Trail continues along Cheaha Creek. A small campsite is located on your right, next to the creek and not very far from where the Skyway Loop Trail splits off. Within a few minutes, the trail and creek will head NE and the trail will ascend above the creek. At .5 mile, reach the Devil's Den, where a wooden ramp and steps descend before arriving at Cheaha Falls. This is a popular location for both campers and day hikers, who enjoy the Falls and pools to cool off during hot weather.

Reach another small campsite just above the Falls. At approximately .7 mile, cross a small creek on your left. Another small campsite is located just ahead on your right. The trail turns N at approximately 1.1 miles and leaves the creek. Ascend and swing around a cove at approximately 1.5 miles before ascending and crossing a ridge. The trail then descends and crosses a small creek. Bear right as the trail crosses a second ridge and swings around to cross a third ridge. Descend from this 3rd ridge (good views of Talladega Mountain) and cross Cheaha Creek at approximately 2.4 miles. Reach FS Road 600 at 3.0 mile. Cross the road and come to a trail sign just ahead. Cross a small creek before coming to the paved road, which leads to Cheaha State Park to the north and soon ends after traveling south approximately 1 mile. A parking area to your right would eliminate having to retrace your hike by having a second vehicle at this location.

Cross the road and swing S before reaching the Turnipseed Hunter Camp at 4.0 miles. This is a large area used as a hunter camp during hunting season. From here the trail turns SE and reaches the Cheaha Wilderness boundary at 4.4 miles. The last mile of the trail ascends, rather steeply, to intersect the Pinhoti Trail on top of Talladega Mountain. Caney Head Shelter is located only a few yards to your left. The Odum Scout Trail continues straight ahead while the Pinhoti Trail follows the ridgetop of Talladega Mountain.

Lake Chinnabee is easy to reach by driving to Cheaha State Park and following the signs.

SKYWAY LOOP TRAIL *Moderate*

This 6 mile trail branches off from the Chinnabee Silent Trail and winds up at Adams Gap on Forest Service Road 600. From the campground at Lake Chinnabee, follow the Chinnabee Silent Trail along Cheaha Creek. The sign for the 2 miles Lakeshore Trail is located approximately 50 yards down the trail. This trail follows the shoreline of Lake Chinnabee as a 2 miles loop. Continue straight and reach the sign for the Skyway Loop Trail another 100 yards down the trail.

Bear right at the sign and cross Cheaha Creek by way of large rocks. The trail ascends and makes its way along a ridge, with Cheaha Creek below on your left. The trail will cut back to your right at approximately 1/2 mile and make its way along the ridge before switching back to your left and heading S. Cross two very small creeks, with a small campsite, and reach Forest Service Road 645 at approximately 1.1 mile. Cross the road and soon reach a very overgrown area with briars. I found two small metal signposts, which helped in navigating through the overgrowth. This is the only bad section of the trail, but a Cheaha Wilderness map and compass are needed if you are going to hike this trail. After briefly ascending from the overgrowth, across FS Road 645F. The trail soon makes a switchback to your left; but, this is hard to find due to downed trees and bulldozer tracks, After several switchbacks, reach Hubbard Creek at approximately 2.3miles. This area near the creek is suitable for camping and the creek is large enough to provide a water source. Any water should be boiled, chemically treated or filtered before use. The trail crosses Hubbard Creek and ascends around a ridge. Upon reaching the top of the small ridge, bear left and pick up the trail again on your right. At approximately 2.7 miles, the trail reaches a FS Road but remains to the left as it continues along the ridge. This part of the trail will provide views of the Talladega Mountain ridge to the south. Cross old FS Road at approximately 3.1 miles and descend. The trail will cut back to the left at approximately 3.6 miles and then back to the right before ascending. Cross an old FS Road at 4.0 miles and descend. The trail will wind around three ridges before descending and making its way through an overgrowth area. At approximately 4.8 miles, cross two creeks where the smaller one merges with the larger. You will soon cross two more small creeks and gradually ascend (heading south). Cross another creek at approximately 5.2 miles and continue to gradually ascend. Cross an old FS Road at 5.9 miles and ascend before reaching FS Road 600 and Adams Gap at 6.0 miles. The Pinhoti Trail crosses the road here. To the right, it is 6.0 miles to Clairmont Gap and to the left, it is 5.5 miles to Caney Head Shelter and 11 miles to Cheaha State Park facilities. FS Road 600 leads north approximately 6 miles to intersect the paved CR 42 running through Cheaha State Park.

Whereas the Chinnabee Silent Trail is a favorite for those camping at Lake Chinnabee and day use folks, the Skyway Loop Trail receives very little traffic and will provide a hike with variable terrain and lots of solitude. I strongly suggest carrying map, compass, snacks and water.

LAKESHORE TRAIL *Easy*

This 2 miles loop trail follows the shoreline of Lake Chinnabee. The trail starts approximately 50 yards from the trailhead sign for the Chinnabee Silent Trail located at the south end of the lake. Cross Cheaha Creek by way of large rocks and follow the trail as it follows the shoreline of the lake. After the trail swings around to the left at approximately 1 mile, you come to the small dam. Cross the creek just below the dam. Be careful when crossing the rocks. The trail then follows the shoreline back to the right. Cross another creek at approximately 2.0 miles and continue to follow the shoreline. The trail ends back at the camping area. There are some uphill areas and 3 creek crossings: but leisurely walked, this trail is not difficult.

BANKHEAD NATIONAL FOREST

The Bankhead National Forest is located in northwestern Alabama and encompasses some 179,000 acres. Picturesque rock bluffs, flowing streams, canyons, waterfalls and wilderness solitude all make this a great area for hiking and camping, as well as other outdoor activities.

Lake Lewis Smith covers an area of over 41,000 acres and provides a variety of recreation from boating to swimming to lakeside camping. Brushy Creek Lake offers more primitive camping with picnic facilities. The Sipsey River offers a great place for canoe outings and the Sipsey Wilderness allows the avid hiker to explore beautiful canyons and waterfalls.

Developed camping facilities are located at Corinth and Houston as well as the newer Clear Creek Recreation Area on Smith Lake. Brushy Creek offers primitive camping.

Bankhead Forest - Thompson Creek Area

RAVEN TRAIL (2.5 Miles) *Easy*

This easily marked trail is located at the Clear Creek Recreation area on Smith Lake. The trailhead begins across the road from the parking area. The trail heads in a SW direction, gradually ascending. Within a matter of minutes, come to a small waterfall, where the trail cuts back to the right and follows the ridge for a short distance. As the trail swings around the ridge and heads S, a short trail to the right leads to the Oak Leaf Shelter and the lake. Continue S and soon come to a second junction. You may hike the remaining trail in either direction from here. I continued on the lower section by turning right. The trail winds around the ridge, passing more rocky overhang "Rockhouse" structures. The second rockhouse structure allows the trail to pass under the overhanging cliff. At approximately 1 mile, cross the paved road leading to several camping areas. The trail continues to ascend gradually and makes its way back to the paved road not far from the park entrance. Views of Smith Lake can be found at several points. Cross the paved road and hike first in a NE direction and then SW along the ridge. The trail then gently descends and intersects the lower section at the junction mentioned earlier. You can retrace the first part of the trail or take the spur trail leading down to the bicycle trail and lake. This trail is nicely marked, offers a variety of terrain with views of the lake, waterfalls and rockhouses, and can be easily hiked. The Clear Creek Recreation Area can be reached by taking Hwy 195 north of Jasper and County Road 27 for approximately 8 miles. Forest signs make it easy to follow, although construction on County Road 27 presently forces a well marked detour.

SIPSEY RIVER RECREATION AREA TRAIL *Easy*

This picturesque trail starts at the day use area on County Road 60 just south of the Sipsey Wilderness. It leads S along the west bank of the Sipsey River. This area is a popular "put-in place" for canoe enthusiasts. Although not very long, the trail winds along the canyon wall past rock cliffs and an occasional waterfall. After passing by a small pavilion area, the trail continues along the river before ending at approximately 1.0 mile. Future proposals for the Bankhead Forest include extending this trail for several miles toward

One of many waterfalls in the Bankhead Forest

Smith Lake, into which the Sipsey River flows.

BRUSHY CREEK *Easy/Moderate*

The Brushy Creek area lies within the Bankhead, just east of the Sipsey Wilderness. There are actually two trails that skirt the west side of the lake near the picnic day use area. The hard surface trail follows the shoreline for approximately 1/4 mile and ends at the dam. A second trail ascends to the rock cliffs above before following the cliffs. It descends to the paved trail at the dam. You could continue along the canyon wall, but the trail becomes overgrown.

Another trail is located across the Lake. This can be reached by crossing Brushy Creek below the dam. This trail, shown on the Bankhead Forest map, is somewhat overgrown however. Brushy Creek also has a small campground area besides the picnic facilities. The area can be reached by turning north onto State HWY 33 in Double Springs. Drive 11 1/2 miles and turn right on County Road 63. After .4 mile turn left (east) onto Forest Service Road 245. After 3 miles, County Road 245 will turn right and reach Brushy Creek in another 1.7 miles.

WILDERNESS TRAILS

There are two wilderness areas within Alabama's national forests. The Sipsey Wilderness consists of 25,988 acres and is located in northwest Alabama within the Bankhead National Forest. The Cheaha Wilderness consists of 7,490 acres and is located within the Talladega National Forest in east-central Alabama.

The 1964 Wilderness Act defines wilderness as an area: "where the earth and its community of life are untrammeled by man..." "Which generally appears to have been affected primarily by the forces of nature with the imprint of man's work substantially unnoticeable..." "Where man himself is a visitor who does not remain..." "Which has outstanding opportunities for solitude or a primitive and unconfined type of recreation... "

Wilderness areas are managed to restore and preserve the natural ecological environment with opportunities for solitude and primitive recreation by man. Cutting of live trees and removal of plantlife is illegal. Visitors to the areas are requested to carry out all trash and erase campsite fire areas before leaving. Motorized vehicles are not allowed in wilderness areas. All water not carried into the area should be treated by purification tablets, filtering devices or boiled. Be aware of ticks, stinging insects, poisonous snakes and plants (poison ivy, etc.).

Items suggested to take with you should include food and water, map, compass, whistle and knife. Be aware of weather conditions that may change. Hike with a friend and leave your travel plans with someone before leaving home.

31.

SIPSEY WILDERNESS

The Sipsey Wilderness area is located in northwestern Alabama where the Appalachian Plateau, the Cumberland Plateau and the Coastal Plain merge. Here, one will find a diversity of vegetation as well as terrain. Within the wilderness are hardwood forests, swift streams, waterfalls and gorges, sandstone cliffs and a variety or plant and animal life.

The original 12,726 acres were created in 1975 by the National Wilderness Preservation Act and later expanded in October of 1988 to encompass 25,986 acres. One should be aware of a number of hazards when venturing into wilderness areas. These include poisonous snakes prevalent to the area, gorge areas being subject to flash flooding, and changing weather conditions.

Here in the Sipsey Wilderness can be found the isolation and solitude that make up the "wilderness experience." A number of trails lead into the area from several trailheads. Before venturing into the forest however, it is suggested that you take along a number of items. These should include area maps, a compass, whistle, food and water. These can usually be purchased at any outdoor store. Please help protect the wilderness areas by using only dead wood for campfires and packing out all debris and garbage. Erase any evidence of campfire areas. Hike with a friend and leave plans before leaving home.

TRAIL #200 *Easy*

The trailhead for this wilderness trail is located at the eastern end of the bridge over the Sipsey River on county road 60. It can also be hiked from the northern terminus on Forest Road 224, where it crosses Borden Creek. (the road is closed to vehicles past the bridge since the wilderness expansion)

From the parking area at the bridge, walk under the bridge to

Sipsey Wilderness - Trail #200

34.

the trailhead. The trail parallels the Sipsey River for the first .5 mile to where Borden Creek merges with the Sipsey. Here, the trail bears right and follows Borden Creek NE. (Trail #209 begins across the creek and follows the Sipsey River for nearly 7 miles) Continue along the eastern bank of Borden Creek. At approximately 1.2 miles, the trail veers north for a short distance before crossing an unnamed creek and heading W.

At approximately 1.7 miles, the trail veers north and passes along high bluffs and ledges before ending near the bridge on FR 224. I found this last mile of the trail to be much more interesting than the first part due to the rocky bluffs and cliffs. At one point, the trail passes through a rock formation.

TRAIL #201 *Easy*

This trail starts at the trailhead and parking area on county road 60 approximately 5 miles west of the Sipsey River Recreation area.

From the trailhead, hike north for approximately .3 mile before reaching a junction with Trail #202 (this trail leads NW approximately 2.9 miles, where it intersects with Trail #209 on the Sipsey River).

Trail #201 continues N for another 2 miles, where it intersects Trail #209 (this trail descends approximately .5 mile to the Sipsey River and crosses before continuing SE for another 6.5 miles).

At approximately 2.4 miles, just past the junction with Trail #209, the trail forks. The right fork leads to a dead end on a bluff above the river. Bear left at the fork. The trail soon descends along and around the ridge for another .5 mile before ending at the Sipsey River. There is a small secluded campsite here.

TRAIL #202 *Easy*

This trail leaves Trail #201 .3 mile from the trailhead and parking area on county road 60. From the junction, the trail wanders along a long ridge for approximately 2.5 miles. The only interesting part of the trail is an old cemetery on your right approximately .8 mile from the start.

Sipsey Wilderness - Trail #204

At approximately 2.5 miles, the trail descends to the Sipsey River. Cross the river and pick up Trail #209.

This trail, in combination with trails #209 and #201, provides a loop hike of approximately 10 miles.

TRAIL #204 *Easy*

Like trail #205, the trailhead for #204 is located on FR 224. When the Sipsey Wilderness was expanded in 1988, this part of the road became inaccessible by motor vehicle. It is approximately 4 miles to Thompson Creek on FR 224 & FR 208, and approximately 4 miles to Borden Creek on FR 224.

The first .6 mile is a wide trail leading SE along the ridge. Here, the wide trail will bear right, descending into the canyon. With a nice waterfall and the state's largest tree, a 500 year old 150' poplar, it is easy to see why this canyon area has been so popular for hikers. The trail into the canyon will parallel the creek and eventually intersect Trail #209 and the Sipsey River.

The main trail becomes narrow and continues SE along the ridge for approximately .5 mile before gradually descending and making several switchbacks around the ridge. At approximately 2.0 miles, the trail descends beside a small waterfall and rockhouse on your left. The next .4 mile continues to descend along the ridge before intersecting with trail #209.

From the junction of trails #204 and #209, the hiker may continue W on trail #209 and N on trail #206 to the Thompson Creek trailhead and parking area. A second option would be to hike SE on trail #209 and then N on trail #200 to the bridge on Borden Creek and parking area. Of course, the third option would be to hike SE on trail #209 and then N on trail #200 to County Road 60 trailhead and parking area.

TRAIL #205 *Easy*

The trailhead for this trail, like that of Trail #204, is located on FR 224. This area, however, is inaccessible by motor vehicle since the Sipsey Wilderness expansion in 1988. The closest parking area is

FR 208 at Thompson Creek, which is 3 miles west of the trailhead.

From FR 224, the trail basically follows the ridgeline between Whiteoak Hollow and Bee Branch Creek. The trail narrows a couple times but for the most part, it is mainly a wide trail and easy to hike.

The last quarter mile is a moderate descent down a rocky watershed to a junction with Trail #206. This trail and Trail #206 could be used along with FR 208 for a loop hike.

TRAIL #206 *Easy*

This trail follows Thompson Creek south, where it merges with several other creeks to form the Sipsey River. The trailhead is located on FR 208, which runs along the northern edge of the Sipsey Wilderness. (East of Thompson Creek is closed to vehicle traffic)

The trail runs south and parallels Thompson Creek briefly before turning E and crossing a smaller creek. It then returns to parallel Thompson Creek with a rocky bluff on your left. At approximately 1.0 mile, reach an area on your right suitable for camping. A short distance later, the trail turns E and crosses another small creek. At approximately 1.7 miles, the trail crosses a small creek area and cuts back SW. Here, a very short spur trail ascends up to a waterfall and the rocky cliffs above the creek.

At approximately 2.5 mile, Quillan Creek (after merging earlier with Hubbard Creek) merges with Thompson Creek to form the Sipsey River. Reach a small area at approximately 2.8 miles suitable for camping. At 2.9 mile, an unmarked (except for a scar on a tree on your left) and hard to recognize trail on your left ascends up a rocky drainage to the ridge above the canyon. (this is Trail #205, which follows the ridge to FR 224)

Just past this trail junction, you will intersect Trail #209. A signpost notates that Trail #209 crosses the Sipsey River here enroute to its junction with Trail #201. (Trail #209 continues SE along the Sipsey River for approximately 6.5 miles) Trail #206 is a great hike in Spring when the flowers are blooming. It can be hiked in conjunction with the other trails to make a nice backpacking trip in the wilderness.

TRAIL #209 *Easy*

This is the longest of the wilderness trails and perhaps the most interesting. The southern terminus is located by hiking trail #200 north from the Sipsey River Recreation Area on county road 60 for .5 mile. The northern terminus is located .5 mile west of the Sipsey River at a junction with Trail #201.

The trail follows the Sipsey River for 6.5 miles from Borden Creek before crossing the river and ascending to its junction with Trail #201. Along the route, you will find numerous side canyons, rock bluffs and waterfalls.

After crossing Borden Creek, the trail heads NW parallel to the river. At approximately .5 mile, reach a small canyon on your right, with a small campsite. Just ahead and near the river is another campsite area. A short distance ahead, the trail will bear right before crossing Fall Creek near a rockhouse and waterfall.

Approximately 1.2 miles, the trail passes along the base of the canyon wall and another waterfall. At approximately 1.5 miles, the trail and river get farther away from the canyon walls. After crossing a small creek, the trail continues far a short distance on an old roadbed.

At 2.2 miles, cross another small creek. The trail and river soon turn SW at approximately 2.5 miles.

Reach a campsite area large enough for a group on your right soon after the trail turns SW, and another smaller campsite along the river ahead at 2.9 miles. At approximately 3.0 miles, the trail and river cut back to the NW. Pass by canyon walls for a short distance before crossing a watershed on your right at approximately 3.6 miles. Here, the river turns W.

At 4.1 miles, the river turns to the N. Reach a junction with Trail #202 at 4.4 miles (the sign was missing, but the post was still in place when I hiked this trail). Trail #202 descends to the ridgetop across the river and winds SW for 2.9 miles to intersect Trail #201. There is another small campsite near the trail junction and another

Sipsey Wilderness - Trail #209

just ahead a short distance.

Cross a creek at 5.1 miles, with a camping area just ahead. A small creek winds its way through the lowland before entering the river.

Reach a junction with Trail #204 at 6.0 miles. (This trail ascends to the ridge and continues NE along the ridge to its trailhead on FR 224. The popular Bee Branch area is reached by taking this trail). Another campsite is located beside the river on your left.

At 6.5 miles, cross Bee Branch Creek, with campsites on each side of the junction with the Sipsey River. The river quickly turns to the W for a short distance. Reach another campsite area at 7.0 miles and also a campsite area at 7.5 miles, where the river turns S.

At 8.0 miles, cross a small creek and reach another campsite just ahead. At 8.5 miles, reach a junction with Trail #206, which continues N for 2.9 miles to Thompson Creek bridge on FR 208. Trail #209 crosses the river here and continues on your right after crossing. The next .5 mile ascends before reaching Trail #201.

SIPSEY WILDERNESS ROADS *Easy*

The expansion of the wilderness in 1988 entailed the closing of several forest service roads to vehicle traffic. These roads also provide a great opportunity to hike through the Sipsey area for those folks who may desire a more moderate terrain without rocky and narrow trails to navigate. They also provide a quiet, secluded trip through the wilderness for those wishing solitude.

Forest Road #224 turns off of county road 60 approximately .5 mile W of Ala. State Hwy 33 and 3 miles E of the Sipsey River. It is closed to vehicles at the bridge crossing Borden Creek. It leads NW for approximately 5 miles before intersecting Forest Road #208. Trailheads for both 204 and 205 trails are located on this road. Another 3 miles on Forest Road #208 will lead to the bridge over Thompson Creek and parking area.

Forest Road #208 runs W from Ala. State Hwy 33 along the NE edge, through the expanded wilderness area and along the NW edge of the wilderness, before intersecting Forest Road #203. Approximately 7 miles of the road are closed from the junction with Forest Road #229 to the bridge over Thompson Creek.

Forest Road #229 runs along the NE side of the wilderness and intersects Forest Road #208. From the junction with #208, approximately 3 miles of this road leading S through the wilderness expansion area is closed to vehicles.

Forest Road #223, connecting #213 and #208, runs through the northern part of the wilderness for approximately 3 miles.

CHEAHA WILDERNESS

The Cheaha Wilderness area lies within the Talladega National Forest and surrounds a portion of the southernmost extension of the Appalachian Mountain chain. It is named for nearby Cheaha Mountain, the highest point in Alabama at 2,407'. Here, one can find solitude within the forest or atop the mountain ridges, waterfalls and numerous panoramic views of the area.

The 7,490 acre wilderness area was created in 1983. Several trails crisscross the area including the Pinhoti trail, which extends over 80 miles from north to south through the Talladega National Forest. Animal life in the area includes deer, opossum, rabbit, squirrel, bobcat, weasel, and songbirds, owls, hawks, wild turkey, dove, and harmless snakes along with the poisonous copperhead, cottonmouth and timber rattlesnake.

When visiting any wilderness area, one should plan on taking several items, including food and water, area map, compass, whistle. Remember to leave the area as you found it; use only dead wood for campfires and erase any evidence of campfire areas. Carry out all debris and garbage. Hike with a friend and leave travel plans with someone at home.

ODUM SCOUT TRAIL *Moderate*

The trailhead for this trail is located off FR 650 near Pyriton, near the southern edge of the Cheaha Wilderness. After crossing the creek near the trailhead sign, bear right. You will ascend the ridge via hand rails and concrete stairs, with High Falls on your right. The stairs and hand rails were built by the Boy Scout organization when they built the 10 mile trail across Talladega Mountain. After passing High Falls, the trail makes a long gradual ascent up Cedar Mountain. At approximately 3.3 miles, reach the crest of the ridge with views of Shinbone Ridge to the east and the long ridge of Talladega Mountain

Odum Scout Trail - High Falls

on the west. Reach a junction with the Nubbin Creek Trail at approximately 3.7 miles.

This trail makes its way along the eastern side of the mountain before ascending along Mill Shoal Creek to Nubbin Creek road. Continue past the junction and pass east of Odum Point, the highest point in the Cheaha Wilderness at 2,342'.

Reach the Caney Head Shelter and the junction with the Pinhoti and Chinnabee Silent Trails at 4.7 miles. The Odum Scout Trail will merge with the Pinhoti Trail as it winds along the top of Talladega Mountain to Cheaha State Park. The Chinnabee Silent Trail descends to the W side of the mountain and leads 6 miles to Lake Chinnabee campground and lake.

NUBBIN CREEK TRAIL *Moderate*

Due to its location, this trail doesn't receive as much traffic as the nearby trails; but in conjunction with one of the other trails nearby, it would make for a very nice hike. The trailhead is located on Nubbin Creek road approximately 2 miles after turning off County Road 31 south of Mannings Chapel. County Road 31 can be reached by turning off Alabama Highway 49 just south of its junction with Alabama 281 near Cheaha State Park.

The trail starts in an overgrown area just off the road. It soon ascends along the south bank of Mill Shoal Creek. After crossing a small creek, bear left and back to the right before entering the Cheaha Wilderness. Ascend moderately and reach a series of cascading waterfalls on Mill Shoal Creek at approximately 1 mile. The trail follows the ridge before ascending again to cross a small creek. Continue NE along the ridge, ascending gradually. The trail then swings around the ridge and soon heads in a SW direction.

At approximately 3.0 miles, the trail swings left (S). The Cave Creek Trail will intersect the Nubbin Creek Trail at this point. (The Cave Creek Trail will ascend to your right back along the ridge). This area was not marked when I hiked the two trails. Hikers can hike the Cave Creek Trail to the parking area on Ala. highway 281 near the entrance to Cheaha State Park.

At approximately 3.5 miles, the trail crosses Mill Shoal Creek near its beginning at Little Caney Head. The trail will continue to ascend, reaching Parker High Point, elevation 2,232'. This area is dominated by large boulders and rock formations. At 4.0 miles, reach the junction with the Odum Scout Trail. To the right 1 mile is Caney Head Shelter and the junction with the Pinhoti and Chinnabee Silent Trails. To the left 3.7 miles is the southern terminus of the Odum Scout Trail and High Falls.

CAVE CREEK TRAIL *Easy*

This new trail originates within Cheaha State Park and intersects the Nubbin Creek Trail within the Cheaha Wilderness area. It basically parallels the Pinhoti Trail, but provides views of the Talladega Forest east of Talladega Mountain. I have included the trail within the Cheaha Wilderness, since the major part of the trail lies within the Wilderness area.

Parking is available where the Talladega Scenic Drive curves sharply to the right just below Cheaha State Park. A short path at the end of the parking area leads to the trailhead sign. Another short trail leads to the Pinhoti trail.

The Cave Creek trail heads south along Talladega Mountain. The trail crosses numerous small watersheds as it winds its way through a mixed hardwood and pine forest. Reach a sign at the Cheaha Wilderness boundary at approximately 1.3 mile. Continue south until the trail turns sharply back to the right at approximately 2.0 miles. A large rock outcrop on your left provides a nice place to rest and affords very good views of the surrounding area.

The trail will ascend approximately 75 yards and cross an old trail. Continue straight. (To the right and approximately 100 yards uphill is a very small and secluded campsite). The trail gradually descends and reaches Cave Creek at approximately 2.3 miles. Cross the creek by way of large rocks and bear left as the trail ascends along the ridge. After a brief descent, the trail will gradually ascend . Reach a sign at approximately 3.2 miles. A short 150 yard connector trail leads R to intersect the Pinhoti Trail. (A 3.5 miles hike N on the Pinhoti Trail will complete a loop back to Cheaha State Park)

Continue S on the Cave Creek Trail, gradually descending. At 4.0 miles, intersect the Nubbin Creek Trail. To the left, it is approximately 3 miles to the Nubbin Creek trailhead. Continuing straight, the Nubbin Creek Trail continues S along the ridge before intersecting the Odum Scout Trail.

Placing alternate transportation at either the Nubbin Creek trailhead or the Odum Scout trailhead will allow for a " one-way" hike rather than backtracking on the Cave Creek Trail. Parking at the Turnipseed Hunter Camp on the Chinnabee Silent Trail offers yet another optional hike. Hiking the Cave Creek and Nubbin Creek Trails allow the hiker a more secluded walk, as the Pinhoti Trail is more heavily traveled.

STATE PARK
TRAILS

From short walking trails to overnight backpacking trails, Alabama's State Park system offers many trails to the hiker. One can enjoy a peaceful walk along a lakeside trail, hike to a canyon overlook, hike along the ridge to panoramic views of the valleys below or hike through backwoods to secluded campsites.

Cheaha State Park offers short trails to fantastic overlooks. Buck's Pocket State Park offers secluded trails leading to a canyon overlook, rock formations or along a stream. Oak Mountain State Park, the largest in the state, offers over 33 miles of backpacking trails. Some 17 state parks offer a variety of trails to explore. I have only included those state parks that offer more than just a very short nature walk of less than a mile, unless that trail leads to a panoramic view such as a waterfall or mountain overlook, such as at Cheaha State Park. The smaller parks with only nature trails or paved trails have been excluded from this publication, since I am mainly writing on hiking trails. For the beginning hiker or local outdoor enthusiasts, these shorter trails however may be very enjoyable.

With 24 state parks throughout the state, 17 of them offering some type of trail, the chance to enjoy one or our state parks is not far away. The address for information on Alabama State Parks is listed in the back of this publication.

Cheaha State Park

CHEAHA STATE PARK

This scenic mountain park offers panoramic views from atop its 2,700 acre retreat. Cheaha Mountain, at 2,407', is Alabama's highest point, surrounded by the Talladega National Forest. Facilities include a resort inn, restaurant, chalets, cottages, group lodge, campground and HIKING TRAILS.

Bald Rock, Pulpit Rock and Rock Garden Trails are all very short trails leading to fantastic overlooks while the Lake Trail descends from the cliff area to Lake Cheaha below. The Pinhoti Trail passes through the park and the Cave Creek Trail originates in the park before entering the Cheaha Wilderness area. Several other trails in the area make this a great location for day hikes or backpacking. Cheaha Lake and Lake Chinnabee provide camping facilities.

Cheaha State Park is located south of 1-20 near the cities of Oxford and Anniston. Turn onto U.S. Highway 431 and go approximately 3.5 miles to the sign for Cheaha State Park. Turn right and drive along the Talladega Scenic Drive for approximately 12 miles to the park.

BALD ROCK TRAIL *Easy*

This short trail begins at the end of the parking area near Bald Rock Lodge. The wide rocky path leads approximately 1/4 mile (the park map says 1/2 mile) to an overlook area with large boulders. Great views of Anniston to the north and the Talladega Forest below can be seen. Use extreme caution when near the ledge areas as there are no fences or ropes to restrain you.

PULPIT ROCK TRAIL *Easy*

This short trail begins at the parking area on the paved park road. Descend down a rocky trail for a short distance before crossing a small creek. Continue along the ridge to your left and reach a large rock outcrop. Great views are afforded of Talladega to the west and the Talladega Forest below. Cheaha Lake (elevation 1,264') can also be seen below. You may see some folks rappelling as this is a favorite area for rappelling enthusiasts.

Use extreme caution and closely watch smaller children, as there are no fences or restraining ropes near the edge.

ROCK GARDEN TRAIL *Easy*

This very short trail begins at the end of the paved road leading down to cabins 1 & 2 (parking space nearby for the Pulpit Rock Trail). Walk down the paved drive. The trail begins at the end of the drive and descends approximately 100 yards (the park map says 1/4 mile) to a group of large boulders. The views of the Talladega Forest below and the Talladega Mountain area are simply fantastic. Cheaha Lake can be seen below. (The Lake Trail descends from the Rock Garden Trail to Cheaha Lake) A short hike to nearby Pulpit Rock should be made while you are at Cheaha. It also affords outstanding views.

Please use caution when near the edge as there are no fences or restraining ropes. Smaller children should be closely watched.

LAKE TRAIL *Strenuous*

This very steep and rocky trail branches off of the Rock Garden Trail and descends to Cheaha Lake below. It is very easy to follow, with blue markings on numerous rocks and trees. From near the overlook area, the trail descends steeply. The upper part of the trail is dominated by large rocks. At approximately 1/2 mile, the trail leaves the cliff area and continues descending along the ridge. Near the bottom, cross a small creek flowing into the creek on your left. The remainder of the trail parallels the later creek to Lake Cheaha.

This trail is very steep and should not be attempted by anyone not in good physical condition. (The sign near Cheaha Lake states "Mountain Trail" while the sign at the top states "Lake Trail") Hiking either direction is strenuous.

DESOTO STATE PARK

This nearly 5,000 acre park sits atop Lookout Mountain, 8 miles northeast of Fort Payne. Facilities include a picnic and playground area, cabins, chalets, a lodge (motel-restaurant), Campground swimming pool, tennis courts and HIKING TRAILS. Nearby attractions include Desoto Falls, Little River Canyon, Sequoyah Caverns and Weiss Lake. Attractions within 50 miles of the park include Noccalula Falls in Gadsden, Lake Guntersville State Park, Buck's Pocket State Park, Russell Cave National Monument and Chattanooga, Tennessee with Ruby Falls and several other worthwhile attractions.

Desoto Falls is located 7 miles from the information center and Little River Canyon is only 10 miles south of the information center. The Rhododendron and Mountain Laurel make late Spring a beautiful time to visit the park. The West Fork of Little River runs through the park and provides a nice mountain stream with hiking trails paralleling the stream.

Desoto State Park is located east of Interstate 59. Turn onto Al. Hwy 35 at the Ft. Payne, Rainsville exit. After merging with U.S. Highway 11, which runs through Ft. Payne, turn right at the sign in downtown and continue on highway 35. Turn left onto County road 89, which leads to the park.

WHITE (Deep Woods) TRAIL *Easy*

This is the longest of the main park trails and has a number of access points along its route, enabling one to walk sections of the trail rather than the whole trail. The first half of the trail is more secluded while the remainder of the trail east of County Road 89 runs close to the swimming pool, picnic area and numerous cottages along the stream. I am describing the trail beginning in the NW corner of the park.

The trail starts approximately 75 yards N of the western park entrance. From the road, head E and soon ascend. After crossing a clearcut area with power lines, the trail continues to ascend to the right. Reach the park road leading to the wilderness camp area at

DeSoto State Park - West Fork of Little River

approximately 1/4 mile. Cross the road and intersect the ORANGE trail in less than 100 yards. The trail quickly enters a thickly forested area and then an area with larger pine trees as it swings to the NE. Reach the park road running through the wilderness camp area at 1/2 mile.

After crossing the road, the trail makes a switchback and heads SE before reaching a clearing at approximately 3/4 mile. Notice a sign for the Deep Woods Trail. Bear left on the dirt road for approximately 100 yards. Another sign at this point directs the hiker to the right. The next part of the trail passes over and through a number of rock formations before it reaches County Road 89 near the northern park entrance. A short spur trail near the end leads to the paved park road close to the information center building.

The next 1 1/2 miles of the trail run close to park facilities and along the west fork of Little River. After crossing County Road 89, the trail passes near the tennis courts and soon passes between a small creek and the swimming pool. A footbridge crosses the creek with a spur trail that intersects the YELLOW trail. Soon after passing the swimming pool area, the WHITE and YELLOW trails merge briefly. After approximately 50 yards, bear R and ascend steeply. The WHITE trail reaches the picnic area. The trail picks up again to the left and downhill 30 yards from the end of the rock building. (Another spur trail leads downhill to intersect the YEL-LOW Trail)

Descend from the picnic area and cross a footbridge over Indian Falls. (A spur trail on the R leads approximately 100 yards to County Road 89) After crossing the footbridge, the trail forks (the YELLOW Trail descends to the stream; a spur trail on the R ascends to rental cottages) Take the "middle" trail, pass 2 cottages, and bear R when the trail splits again. Ascend and pass more cabins before descending. A spur trail soon descends L to intersect the YELLOW Trail. (Several connecting trails in this area allow the hiker to walk parts of both the YELLOW and WHITE trails) An-other spur trail on the R ascends to the cottages. Pass Lodge Falls on your right at approximately 2.3 miles. More connector trails lead down to the YELLOW trail along the river. Continue to follow the white markers as you pass half a dozen more rental cottages. The trail ends at a dirt road at approximately 3 miles. Follow the dirt road (right) past several rental cottages before coming to the Lodge/Motel.

RED (AZALEA CASCADE) TRAIL *Easy*

This "maze" of connecting trails has several access points. Two parking areas on County Road 89 just S of the Country Store, as well as the ORANGE and BLUE trails, provide several points from which to walk the trails. I have chosen the parking area near the Country Store on County Road 89 to begin walking the trail.

From the small parking area, the trail leads W and passes through two large boulders known as Needle Eye Rock. After passing through the rocks, the trail will bear left and soon reach a junction. By taking the trail to the right, you will walk along the ridge and reach a second junction at approximately .2 mile (This is the ORANGE Trail leading to Laurel Falls) From this point, the trail descends down to Laurel Creek. A junction near the creek will allow you to bear left along the creek and swing back to the first junction mentioned earlier. Upon reaching Laurel Creek, cross on a footbridge and bear left along the south side of the creek. This part of the trail will end at County Road 89, but another footbridge will cross the creek and intersect that part of the trail running along the north side of Laurel Creek. Bear right at this point. Another junction soon allows the hiker to bear left and walk back to the original starting point or continue along Laurel Creek before ending at a small parking area on County Road 89.

The total distance of these "connecting" trails is approximately 1 mile. Spring is definitely the best time to walk this trail because of the Azaleas and Mountain Laurel along the creek.

BLUE (CR CAVES) TRAIL *Easy*

This "secluded" trail branches off from the RED trail and intersects the ORANGE trail approximately 1 1/2 miles later.

Near the footbridge crossing Laurel Creek, Follow the blue tree markings and ascend away from the creek. The trail passes through heavy brush and makes its way along the ridge with numerous rock formations on your left. At approximately 1 mile, a spur trail on the right leads to Lost Falls on Laurel Creek. The trail continues near the creek before crossing at approximately 1.4 mile. Cross a large rocky area where the blue markers will be painted on the rocks. Intersect the ORANGE trail. (Walking to your right will lead back towards the campground area; walking straight will lead to the wilderness camping area)

This trail is definitely secluded from the more traveled trails and provides the solitude that some hikers prefer. During wet weather, care should be taken when crossing the rocky areas.

SILVER (CHRISTENSEN) TRAIL *Easy*

This trail is divided into two sections. The first part connects the park campground with the Information Center. The second part runs from the campground to the paved park road NW of the campground. where it intersects the ORANGE Trail. I have chosen to describe the trail from the Information Center; but it may be walked from the park road, or either half walked from the campground.

The trail starts near the end of the parking area (near the park road entrance into the parking area). After a short distance, the trail begins a gradual ascent. Reach the campground area at .4 mile. The trail picks up again on the other side of the pull-in campsite. From the road, the trail continues NW and reaches a junction with the Yellow (Blue Berry Lane) Trail after 150 yards. (This trail connects the SILVER and ORANGE Trails). The SILVER Trail continues NW and reaches the park road and ORANGE Trail at approximately 1.1 miles from the Information Center trailhead. The first part of the trail is more heavily traveled, since it connects the campground with the Information Center and Country Store area. It is more easily walked from the campground to the Information Center since most of it is downhill.

ORANGE TRAIL *Easy*

This 1.9 mile trail runs from the RED Trail to the Wilderness Camping area. Vehicles can be parked in the small parking area on

County Road 89 for the RED Trail, or a small area 1/2 mile NW of the campground entrance on the park road where the ORANGE Trail crosses the road. The road leading to the Wilderness Camping area is locked, with access only for those who are camping at that location. The trail from the park road to the camp area is only .2 mile; so that part of the trail may easily be walked "in & out."

From its junction with the RED Azalea Trail, the ORANGE Trail heads N and soon swings W. At .1 mile, reach a large rock structure on your left and a spur trail just ahead on your right. This short trail leads to the nearby campground. Cross a small creek and continue, reaching another spur trail on your left at .5 mile. (this short trail leads to Laurel Falls, a small falls on Laurel Creek) After crossing a rocky area, the YELLOW (Blue Berry LN) Trail intersects with the ORANGE Trail at approximately .7 mile. (this .4 mile trail leads to the SILVER Trail just W of the campground area) At .9 mile, cross another rocky area and at 1.1 mile, reach a spur trail on your left that leads to Lost Falls, another small falls on Laurel Creek. Reach a junction with the CR CAVES Trail at 1.3 miles. Blue markers on the rocks to your left will mark this trail, which crosses Laurel Creek and later intersects the RED Trail. The ORANGE Trail swings N and reaches the park road at 1.7 miles. The last .2 mile brings you to the Wilderness Camp area. Picnic tables and a small covered pavilion make this a nice rest stop for those who may wish to hike the WHITE Trail back to the Information Center and Country Store area. This would complete a "loop" hike of approximately 3 1/4 miles.

YELLOW (BLUE BERRY LANE) TRAIL *Easy*

This .4 mile trail connects the SILVER Trail near the campground to the ORANGE Trail .2 miles from Laurel Falls. It can be walked as a "connector trail" just mentioned or in conjunction with the ORANGE and BLUE Trails to create a "loop" hike.

GOLD TRAIL *Easy*

This short 250 yard trail connects the campground area to the Country Store and Information Center. Another very short connector trail leads from the south end of the campground to intersect the

ORANGE Trail. These "connector" trails allow those who use the campground easy access to the trails in the park.

YELLOW (DST) TRAIL   *Moderate*

This trail is part of the longer DESOTO SCOUT TRAIL, which runs from the Comer Boy Scout Camp north of the park to an old church near Al. Highway 35 south of the park and near Little River Canyon.

CAVE TRAIL   *Easy*

This is one of two short trails near Desoto Falls, which is located 7 miles northeast of the park information center. After turning off County Road 89 onto the road leading to Desoto Falls, you will drive around several curves in the road. Look for the power lines on your right and a small road with a large boulder blocking the road from vehicle traffic.

The trail traverses the canyon rim for approximately 1/2 mile. The latter part of the trail makes a loop with a nice observation point for a great view of Desoto Falls. Close to where the loop begins, there are a series of caves below the rim but accessible by climbing down approximately 10-15 feet. There is no sign posted, so the caves may be hard to locate.

Close to where the trail begins, there is a side trail to the right that leads to Icebox Cave and also to the Basin Trail.

BASIN TRAIL   *Easy*

This trail begins .2 mile before the Cave Trail. Walk down the dirt road on your right and under the power lines. The trail descends to the West Fork of Little River. After approximately .2 mile, come to a large tree. The trail will descend to your right and reach the river at approximately .4 mile. The remainder of the overgrown trail parallels the river before crossing at approximately .7 mile and ending below Desoto Falls.

JOE WHEELER STATE PARK

This 2,550 acre facility is located in northwest Alabama just off U.S. Highway 72. It offers a resort inn overlooking the Tennessee River, a marina, an 18-hole golf course, developed and primitive Camping, picnic areas, tennis courts and walking trails.

I have included three park trails because they are not what I consider hiking trails; but they are nice walking trails for those who wish to enjoy the other park facilities.

PINE BARK TRAIL   *Easy*

This short .5 mile trail is located near the day use area and tennis courts. It makes a loop and is a nice walking trail with views of the lake.

LAKE TRAIL   *Easy*

This 1.3 mile trail connects the Pine Bark Trail with the Wheeler Loop Trail. It wanders near the Tennessee River for part of the distance. The park map says that this trail makes a loop back to the service road. This may be future intentions, but for now, the trail only connects the Pine Bark and Wheeler Loop trails.

WHEELER LOOP TRAIL   *Easy*

This 1.0 mile loop trail begins near the park lodge and ends at the corner of the tennis court area. There are several uphill and downhill areas, but overall, the trail is moderate to hike. This trail, like the other two, is short but very nice to walk in the Fall and early Spring.

LAKE GUNTERSVILLE
STATE PARK

This beautiful state park encompasses almost 6,000 acres overlooking 66,470 acre Lake Guntersville. The facilities include a resort lodge, lakeview cottages, chalets, a 322 site campground, swimming beach, fishing center, an 18-hole golf course, tennis courts, picnic pavilions, nature center and 12 miles of HIKING TRAILS. Not far away are Monte Sano State Park in Huntsville, Buck's Pocket State Park and Desoto State Park. These parks offer many miles of hiking trails, all within a short driving distance.

I have described only a few of the trails within the park, since the majority of them are short trails. All of the trails can be walked as day hikes.

CUTCHENMINE TRAIL *Easy*

This is an easy to walk trail that makes its way around the shoreline of Lake Guntersville. The trail begins on Alabama highway 227 approximately 1/2 mile north of the Short Creek bridge. From the trail sign located on the highway, descend and cross a small footbridge on your left. You then bear right and basically follow the shoreline SW. After approximately 1/2 mile, the trail will bear left (still following the shoreline) and parallel Short Creek.

After crossing a creek via large rocks, the trail soon ends at approximately 2.0 miles. A large boulder in the middle of the roadbed marks the end of the trail. This old road once led to a coal mine and has been open to the public as a hiking trail since 1967. Since Lake Guntersville is a popular area for bird watching, especially in winter months, this trail may provide good opportunities for spotting waterfowl and birds of prey, such as the eagle and hawk.

TOM BEVILL TRAIL *Moderate*

This 3 mile trail also has a trailhead on Alabama highway 227 just north of the Short Creek bridge. Cross the road after parking on the right side, and ascend steeply for a short distance. The trail will split here. I suggest walking to your left (W), ascending gradually as the trail winds around Ellenburg Mountain. At approximately 1 1/4 mile, ascend for a short distance and descend, as the trail makes its way around to the north side of the mountain.

Reach the paved park road at approximately 2.0 miles and walk along the road to your right for a short distance. Ascend to your right as the trail winds around the east side of the mountain and reaches the junction above highway 227. Descend to the road and the parking area at 3.0 miles.

LICKSKILLET TRAIL *Moderate*

This trail begins on the road, just east of the campground entrance and store. The first 1/2 mile ascends very moderately up Taylor Mountain before intersecting the paved park road leading to the Park Lodge. Cross the road and walk to your right approximately 50 yards. The trail will bear left along the ridge, before descending NE and cutting back to the SE.

At approximately 1 1/2 miles, reach a park service road (to the left, the road leads down to the lake). Cross the road and ascend NE along Baily Ridge. At approximately 2.1 miles, the trail will turn to your right (E) and ascend to the ridge before descending to Alabama highway 227 south of the Town Creek Bridge.

This trail, when combined with the 2 mile Seales Trail, allows the hiker to begin and end at the park campground.

SEALES TRAIL *Easy*

This trail starts at the north end of the campground and follows the shoreline of the lake to the Town Creek bridge on Alabama highway 227. From the campground, the trail makes its way around a hill covered with large boulders. You can spot a number of bluebirds in this area. Continue around a small inlet and reach a larger inlet at approximately 1 1/2 miles. The gravel road on your right leads to the paved park road atop Taylor Mountain. High water may force the hiker to walk up the road and around the low lying area.

The trail then ascends briefly to parallel the lake about 30 feet above the shoreline as it continues along the ridge. Reach the Town Creek bridge at 2.0 miles.

Descend down wooden steps to the road. The Lickskillet trail is located to your right (S) approximately 150 yards down the road. It can be hiked over Taylor Mountain to return to the campground area.

LAKE LURLEEN STATE PARK

This 1,625 acre park is located in western Alabama, 12 miles northwest of Tuscaloosa. The lake was built in 1956, with state park facilities constructed by 1972. The 250 acre lake provides opportunities for fishing, boating, canoeing and swimming. Other facilities include picnic areas, group picnic shelters, playground areas, camping and HIKING TRAILS.

The park can be reached by taking highway 82 north of Tuscaloosa and following the signs. Additional information can be obtained by writing to the park's address in the back of this book, or to the state park headquarters in Montgomery, which provides information on Alabama's State Park system.

LAKESIDE TRAIL   *Easy*

This shoreline trail of approximately 1 1/4 miles begins near the picnic shelter to your left as you go through the entry station. It follows the shoreline before ending at the dam. This is an easy trail to walk, with opportunities to view a number of birds including the blue heron, egrets, belted kingfisher, blue birds, and water fowl including mallard ducks. Upon reaching the dam, you will have to walk back to the starting point or approximately 1/2 mile along a service road, which leads back to the main park road near the entrance to the State Park.

FOOTHILLS TRAIL   *Easy*

This "3 segmented" trail can be hiked from 3 different starting points, which connect along the ridge. I have chosen to describe the trail from "north to south." The trail begins at the end of a paved cul-de-sac across from playing fields approximately .9 mile after crossing the bridge.

The trail heads E for approximately .2 mile before it swings to your right. From here it makes several descents and ascents as it makes its way along the ridge. At approximately .8 mile, reach an intersection. (Walking to your right, the trail will descend approximately .2 mile to reach the paved park road near a small restroom building across from a playground area) Bear left (S) from the intersection. The trail continues to follow the ridge. At approximately 1.1 miles, a spur trail on your left leads down to a camping area. After another 125 yards, cross a junction with another trail and descent. Reach the paved park road at approximately 1.4 miles. The park map lists this trail as approximately 2 1/4 miles in length, but I found the distance to be considerably less.

After the first .2 mile distance, I found what appeared to be another 1/2 mile trail on your left, which lead to a paved road north of the park boundary. This is not considered part of the Foothills Trail on the map however.

Oak Mountain State Park - Peavine Falls

OAK MOUNTAIN STATE PARK

This nearly 10,000 acre park, the largest in the state, offers something for just about everyone. Facilities include fishing lakes, swimming area, canoe & flat bottom boat rental, picnic area, tennis courts, 18 hole golf course, BMX bicycle track, an animal demonstration farm, cabins, campground and over 30 miles of HIKING TRAILS.

Four trails over 5 miles in length, the 1.9 mile Peavine Trail, plus several "connector" trails enable the hiker to choose from a variety of hiking routes. The Peavine Trail begins across from the tennis courts. The four longer trails share a trailhead near the developed campground. While the Foothills trail ends near the picnic area, the other three can be hiked to the Peavine Falls parking lot. Since a number of park visitors drive the unpaved road up to the Peavine Falls area but don't hike the trails, I have described the four longer trails beginning at the NE trailhead near the campground. The trails range from easy to strenuous. Primitive camping is allowed and a number of back-country sites have been included in this trail description. The Double Oak Trail is also used by mountain bikers. Hikers should carry plenty of water as water sources are not reliable.

PEAVINE TRAIL *Strenuous*

This trail begins across the road from the tennis courts and park office. It ascends steeply for the first 1 mile. At approximately .6 mile, the trail intersects with the Foothills Trail. (To the right, it is approximately .6 mile to the end of the Foothills Trail near the picnic area) To the left, the trail makes its way along the ridge and eventually through lower elevation areas before ending near the NE trailhead and main park road.

At 1.0 mile, the Peavine Trail intersects the Double Oak Trail. (To the left .2 mile is a small shelter.) The Double Oak and Peavine Trails merge for the next .7 mile heading SW along a service road.

At approximately 1.7 miles, the Peavine Trail will ascend the ridge on your left, and descend to intersect the Shackleford Point Trail .1 mile before reaching Peavine Falls, a popular attraction in the park. (The Double Oak Trail continues along the forest road and ends at the Peavine Falls parking lot) From the Falls, it is .4 mile to the parking lot.

FOOTHILLS TRAIL   *Moderate*

This trail begins near the country store at the developed campground. After crossing the main park road, continue on the Double Oak Trail approximately 75 yards from the trailhead. The Foothills Trail will bear right, crossing a footbridge. The Shackleford Point Trail will merge with the Foothills Trail for the first 100 yards, before the two trails split.

The Foothills Trail will ascend to your left while the Shackleford Point Trail continues straight ahead. After a short ascent, the trail will follow a ridge and descend into Maggie's Glen at approximately 1 mile. This area is a frequently used back-country campsite. The .4 mile Gorge Trail on your left leads along a small creek before intersecting the Double Oak Trail. The Shackleford Point Trail on your right will lead back to the trailhead or merge briefly before ascending to your left.

Cross the creek and walk through the hollow in a SW direction. Continue through the hollow and over a small hill before descending to and following a small creek. Reach "Old Lake" at approximately 2.0 miles. Cross a footbridge on your left. There is a small campsite on your right by the footbridge. The trail on the right side of the lake leads to a group of rental cabins.

After crossing the footbridge, the trail continues around the lake before reaching the spillway. You will notice some old CCC cabins on the hill above the lake. A forest road leads from the old cabins to the main park road. From the spillway,the trail descends and makes its way through an overgrowth area before arriving at the old primitive campground area at 3.0 miles. This is now a day use area with a pavilion and picnic tables.

From the day use area, the trail will continue along the creek for a short distance before crossing a footbridge. It then winds around the ridge, crosses a small creek and ascends and crosses another ridge. Descend to a park service road at approximately 4.0 miles.

Bear left on the road, crossing a wooden bridge over the creek. (to your right, the road leads a short distance to the main park road)

After crossing the bridge, the trail will continue on your right. A "Yellow-White" connector trail 10 yards further down the road will also bear to the right and ascend steeply to join the Shackleford Point Trail on the ridge above. The park road continues up the ridge to end at the old CCC cabins mentioned earlier.

After bearing right and leaving the service road, the Foothills Trail will cross a footbridge and ascend to a small ridge. Hike along the south side of this ridge and descend to cross a small creek. Ascend again and cross a paved park road at approximately 6.8 miles. (This road leads to the animal rescue service building, where rescued wild animals are cared for) Cross the paved road and ascend before descending to a "ravine" area. The trail to the right descends to the Tree Top Nature Trail and exhibit of injured wildlife unable to be returned to the wild. Continue along the ridge and intersect the Peavine Trail at approximately 7.3 miles. Several small campsites can be found along this area of the trail. (The Peavine Trail leads from the tennis court area on the paved Park road to Peavine Falls, a popular destination for many park visitors) From the intersection with the Peavine Trail, the Foothills Trail will descend from the ridge and end near the picnic area.

This park trail may not be as popular as the other four trails, which end at or near Peavine Falls, but it offers the hiker a variety of terrain and sites.

SHACKLEFORD POINT TRAIL *Moderate*

This trail, like the Double Oak and South Rim Trails, starts at the NE trailhead on the main park road leading to Oak Mountain fishing lake. Walk along the Double Oak Trail for approximately 75 yards. The Shackleford Point Trail and Foothills Trail (this trail started at the campground) will cross the footbridge on your right and head SW. After 100 Yards, these two trails will split. The Shackleford Point Trail will continue SW around the base of the ridge while the Foothills Trail ascends the ridge on your left.

After .8 mile, the trail will bear SE and reach Maggie's Glen at

1.2 miles. This is a popular campsite area. The Foothills Trail intersects the Shackleford Point Trail here, as does the .4 mile Gorge Trail. (This trail leads along the creek before intersecting the Double Oak Trail) Cross the creek and ascend to your left after a short distance. (The Foothills Trail continues straight ahead)

Reach Cove Top Cliff at approximately 1.7 miles. Good views of Hawk Rock and Shackleford Gap can be seen from here. Continue SW along the ridge and reach Shackleford Point, the highest elevation in the park, at 2.4 miles. At approximately 2.5 miles, reach the intersection with the Mt. Top Trail, a connector trail that leads .3 mile to the Double Oak Trail and .7 mile to the South Rim Trail. This, and other connector trails, offer the hiker a variety of walking routes. Continue SW along the ridge and intersect the Double Oak Trail at 3.7 miles. The Yellow-White connector trail on your right will descend from the ridge to intersect the Foothills Trail. From the trail junction, the Double Oak Trail will follow the ridge SW while the Shackleford Point Trail descends between the two ridges. It then follows Peavine Creek SW to Peavine Falls. At approximately 5.1 miles, the short White-Blue connector trail crosses the creek to intersect the South Rim Trail.

Continue to parallel the creek and reach a small footbridge at approximately 6.0 miles. The Peavine Trail will intersect Shackleford Point Trail near the footbridge. To the left and across the creek is Peavine Falls, a popular destination for many park visitors. The South Rim Trail will ascend and follow the back ridge of Double Oak Mountain to the trailhead mentioned earlier. A small campsite can be found on the top of the ridge above the South Rim Trail and Peavine Falls.

From the footbridge at the top of the Falls, the South Rim Trail, which intersects the Shackleford Point Trail at the footbridge, will lead .4 mile to the parking area.

SOUTH RIM TRAIL *Moderate*

This trail shares the same trailhead as the Double Oak and Shackleford Point Trails. From the NE trailhead, the trail quickly ascends for a short distance, before leveling out along a small ridge.

Ascend again along the ridge and reach the Red-Blue connector trail at .8 mile. This short trail descends steeply to intersect the Double Oak Trail.

From the junction, ascend steeply for a short distance before the trail widens and levels out. Near a large boulder area on your left, you may notice a very narrow trail ascending up the ridge. This small trail leads to a nice campsite on top of the ridge. Hawk Rock, a large rock on the side of the ridge, provides an excellent view of the two ridges making up Double Oak Mountain.

Continue on the main trail, as it winds around the ridge. Reach Gum Hollow at 1.3 miles, where the trail bears right and begins its long route along the ridge. This area is a popular campsite area. From the large rocky area where the trail turns SW along the ridge, you can walk to your left (NE) 200 yards and reach a secluded area suitable for camping.

Hiking SW along the ridge, reach Shackleford Gap at 2.0 miles. Here, a large boulder on your right offers a great view of Hawk Rock and the front ridge of Double Oak Mountain. There is a suitable campsite here. At approximately 2.4 miles, a second Red-Blue connector trail will descend to the Double Oak Trail. Continue SW along the ridge and reach the Mt. Top Trail at approximately 3.5 miles. This connector trail leads .4 mile to intersect the Double Oak Trail and .7 mile to intersect the Shackleford Point Trail. To your left, a boulder area along the ridge offers great views of the valley east of the park. A short distance ahead are two campsites on your left.

At approximately 6.1 miles, the short White-Blue connector trail will cross Peavine Creek to intersect the Shackleford Point This trail was not well marked at the time I hiked the trails.

Reach Peavine Falls at approximately 6.3 miles. This area is one of the most popular in the park. A small campsite is located on the ridge before reaching the Falls. A footbridge crosses Peavine Creek above the falls and to the right. The trail continues another .4 mile, as it ascends gradually to the parking area. The South Rim Trail probably offers the most seclusion for the backpacker. Since the trail follows the ridge for most of the length, the backpacker should carry plenty of water.

DOUBLE OAK TRAIL   *Moderate*

This trail shares the same NE trailhead with the South Rim and Shackleford Point Trails. From the trailhead, walk S on a level grade with a small creek on your right. After 75 yards, the Shackleford Point and Foothills Trails will cross a small footbridge over the creek and head SW.

Continue S and cross a small creek before reaching a Red-Blue connector trail at approximately .5 mile. This trail ascends steeply to intersect the South Rim Trail. At .7 mile, the Gorge Trail on your right leads .4 mile along a creek to a junction with the Foothills and Shackleford Point Trails at Maggie's Glen. These trails allow the hiker to make a loop hike back to the trailhead or "switch" to another trail and continue hiking.

The trail will cross a footbridge at 1.3 miles and continue SW between the two ridges that make up Double Oak Mountain. At 1.5 miles, another Red-Blue connector trail on your left will ascend to intersect the South Rim Trail.

Reach the Mt. Top Trail at approximately 2.4 miles. This connector trail will lead right (N) .3 mile to intersect the Shackleford Point trail or left (S) .4 mile to intersect the South Rim Trail. At 3.1 miles, reach the junction with the Shackleford Point Trail. The Yellow-White connector trail will descend NW from the ridge at this point and lead to the Foothills Trail. From this junction, the Double Oak Trail will continue SW along the ridge while the Shackleford Point Trail descends and continues SW between the two ridges.

Reach a small shelter at approximately 4.0 miles. At 4.2 miles, the Peavine Trail on your right descends to its start near the tennis court and day use area. Continue SW along the ridge. At approximately 4.9 miles, the Peavine Trail will ascend on your left and cross the ridge to intersect the Shackleford Point Trail near Peavine Falls. Double Oak Trail will continue straight ahead and arrive at the Peavine Falls parking area at 5.7 miles.

This trail has been authorized for use by mountain bikes as well as hikers. Be aware of bikers while walking this trail.

"CONNECTOR TRAILS"

The connector trails shown on the Oak Mountain trail map allow the hiker to follow any number of routes.

For a variety of terrain from easy to difficult, the following route will make for an interesting hike. Park at the entrance of the forest road located 2.8 miles from the park entrance and 2.8 miles before the entrance road to the developed campground.

Walk down the road approximately 100 yards. (The Foothills Trail will turn right after crossing a wooden bridge) The Yellow/White connector trail is located another 10 yards on your right. It soon ascends, rather steeply, to make its way to the ridge and a junction with the Shackleford Point Trail.

This is the hardest part of the hike. Turn left and hike along the Shackleford Point Trail. It follows the ridge NE before descending to intersect the Foothills Trail. Turn left onto the Foothills Trail near Maggie's Glen and follow it to Old Lake. It will then wind around the edge of the lake and descend beside the spillway. At the bottom, the trail will soon cross the creek on a wooden footbridge and arrive at the day use area with a covered pavilion and picnic tables. This area used to be the primitive campground area.

This hike will encompass ascending,hiking along the ridge with views of the area, and a nice hike through the woods and around a lake. The total distance of the hike will be approximately 5 miles.

Shorter connector trails between the South Rim, Double Oak and Shackleford Point trails will allow a number of different hikes.

WIND CREEK STATE PARK

This 1,400 acre park is located southeast of Alexander City off highway 63. Nestled along the shore of Lake Martin, facilities include a large campground, picnic area, swimming area, marina facility and hiking trails.

The " Yellow" Trail is located near the north picnic area and winds its way through the woods above the lake for approximately 2 1/2 miles. The Alabama Reunion Trail starts behind the parking lot of the registration building on the paved road to the marina area. It makes its way through the woods, crosses highway 128 and follows a forest service road before ending across the highway from the park entrance. The Yellow Trail provides nice views of the lake while the Reunion Trail offers more solitude. A number of forest roads intersect the Reunion Trail; so the hiker should be aware of direction and distance.

"YELLOW TRAIL" *Easy*

The sign for this park trail is located on the paved road leading to the north picnic area. Begin your hike to the left of the creek and walk in a NW direction. After a very short distance, turn right and cross a small footbridge over the creek. Ascend and bear left around a hill, before ascending again in a NE direction. Reach the ridge and bear right on the "Yellow-White" connector trail. After 25-30 yards, the trail will turn left and descend for a short distance. The trail will ascend, then descend, before crossing another small creek. After crossing the small creekbed, the trail will descend gradually in a SE direction towards the lake. Making its way around a small inlet, the trail will swing back in a westerly direction before ascending. Intersect the "Yellow-White" connector trail again. (This trail will lead N along the ridge to the junction mentioned earlier)

Bear left and continue on the Yellow Trail, as it follows the shoreline but remains a short distance from the lake. The trail soon swings back to the NW before ending on the paved road and parking area for the picnic area. You can either walk along the road to your vehicle or hike the two short trails and end at the trailhead area. The "Yellow-Orange" trail ascends approximately 300 yards to intersect the "Yellow-White" connector trail. A few yards to your left is the "Yellow-Blue" trail, which descends approximately 200 yards to the paved road. Walk just a few yards to your right to where you parked.

ALABAMA REUNION TRAIL   *Easy*

This 4 Mile trail is divided by highway 128. The trail starts a short distance down the paved road, next to the camper registration building, which leads to the marina. Park your vehicle in the parking lot at the registration building and walk down the paved road towards the marina. The trail will start just a very short distance on your right.

The first part of the trail makes its way through heavy over-growth and crosses several footbridges over small creekbeds. After crossing the 2nd footbridge, bear right. You will ascend and then descend before crossing another watershed. Notice a sign posted on a tree at 1/2 mile. Cross a 3rd footbridge a short distance further. Upon reaching an old road, bear right and follow the road. The road will soon turn in a SW direction. After approximately 1.0 mile, intersect a forest service road. Bear right onto this road and cross a small stream via rocks before reaching Alabama highway 128.

The trail will pick up again a short distance to your right across the road. The remainder of the trail will follow a forest service road through new growth pine trees. The trail will turn E and gradually ascend. A ravine will be on your right. Several old roads will intersect the main trail. At 1/2 mile, (from Ala. Hwy 128) a sign posted on a tree and a fork in the trail are reached. Bear left (N) and continue, with several old roads crossing the main trail from time to time.

At 1.0 mile (3 miles from start of trail), reach another tree with a sign posted. Here, the trail will turn SE. The trail will soon turn NE and ascend. Pass an old road on your left before reaching a fork in the road. Take the road to the right. A short distance ahead, continue straight where another road bears to the left. Descend and cross a small creek. Reach an "eroded" area. A short distance further, come to another forest road. Turn left on this road and find a

"No Trespassing" sign posted on your left. Reach Ala. Hwy 128 approximately 150 yards ahead. The park entrance is located just across the highway.

This trail would be a nice walk in the FALL, when the leaves turn color. It also offers considerably more solitude than the Yellow Trail located close to the lake and camping areas.

BUCK'S POCKET STATE PARK

This secluded 2,000 acre facility may be the best kept secret among our state Parks. The park offers an observation overlook of the 400 foot deep canyon formed by two creeks, a picnic area near the overlook, improved campsites, primitive camping and several hiking trails in the canyon and to rock structures, including the Point Rock Trail leading from the campground to the overlook.

The park is located some 10 miles north of Geraldine and 23 miles west of Interstate 59 at Ft. Payne. It can also be reached by traveling highway 75 from Albertville and highway 227 from Guntersville. The campground is reached by driving down into the canyon while the picnic area is located near the Overlook. Signs are posted for each area when you reach the Park.

POINT ROCK TRAIL *Moderate*

This trail can be hiked from the canyon below or from the picnic area near the observation overlook. I am describing the trail from its lower trailhead. From the campground walk back along the road to the concrete bridge. The trail starts across the bridge on your left. The first part of the trail follows Little Sauty Creek with water cascades and large boulder formations. At approximately 1 mile, you can note the rock overhang at the end of the short Indian House Trail to your right and above. The trail abruptly crosses over to the left of the creek and soon starts its ascent. The last 1/2 mile or less is a moderate climb to the upper terminus of the trail near the picnic area. The trail has gained some 400' from the canyon floor.

A short walk to your left will take you to the observation overlook of the canyon, well worth the hike. Please use caution. Most of the overlook areas have no fence or restraining device and the distance to the canyon below is several hundred feet. The picnic area and overlook can be reached by the road intersecting the main road leading to the canyon below and campground area.

Buck's Pocket State Park - Point Rock Overlook

INDIAN HOUSE TRAIL *Easy*

This short trail begins beside the concrete drainage pipe just prior to where the road turns right and descends to the canyon floor and campground area. From the road, walk down beside the cascading water and follow the ridge. This is a very short trail (listed as 1/2 mile on trail map) that ends at large rock formations often used by the Cherokee Indians for shelter.

HIGH BLUFF TRAIL *Moderate*

This is another short trail located along the road leading down into the canyon and campground area. A small parking area is located in a sharp curve of the road. The Trail makes its way along the high rock cliffs with a rock overhang and a small stream which flows during the Fall and Winter.

SOUTH SAUTY CREEK TRAIL *Moderate*

This is a 2 1/2 mile dead end trail located "across the stream" from the campground. The trail begins across South Sauty Creek by the concrete bridge. (The Primitive Campground trail begins on the left of the concrete bridge before it crosses the stream) Parking is available on the left after crossing the bridge. From the concrete bridge, the trail leads east along the stream. The trail gradually ascends and makes its way along the cliffs, where several small waterfalls flow during the Fall and Winter months. At approximately 1 1/2 miles, the trail begins to descend and makes its way down to the stream where it dead ends. Four primitive campsites are located at trails end for those who wish to backpack.

PRIMITIVE CAMPGROUND TRAIL *Easy*

This trail starts just past the entrance to the campground before crossing South Sauty Creek. It consists of an old road bed which runs parallel to the creek. During the summer and dry periods, South Sauty Creek actually goes underground due to the canyon floor being honeycombed with limestone caverns beneath the sandstone boulders.

The first 1 1/2 miles of roadbed can be traveled by auto with primitive campsites located on the backwater from Lake Guntersville or you may park in the developed campground area and hike down the road bed. (I do not recommend driving your car down this road, but pickup trucks should have no problem)

From the road, you can see the large sandstone boulders in the creek bed. From the primitive camp area, the road bed continues on your left. Within the first 100 yards, you will pass a couple of wooden outhouses. At approximately 1.7 miles, the trail gets farther away from the backwater and ascends for a short distance via switchbacks.

At 2.0 miles, the road bed becomes smoother after walking over very rocky surface. At 2.3 miles, begin descending. The road bed will level out at approximately 2.6 miles before reaching a paved road at 2.7 miles. Take this paved road RIGHT and reach Morgan's Cove with a nice view of Lake Guntersville. (During the summer months, you may wish to jump in the water)

A T.V.A. access road continues from the end of the parking area along the shore of Lake Guntersville. This would make a hike of approximately 6.0 miles one way. This would be a nice walk in the Fall or early Spring. By driving to Morgan's Cove, you would only have half the hiking distance. During the winter months, this area is very good for viewing Bald Eagles.

MONTE SANO STATE PARK

This scenic park sits atop Monte Sano Mountain, overlooking the city of Huntsville. It covers over 2,100 acres with cliff overlooks of the Huntsville area, forest trails, picnic areas, camping areas and other facilities. You can reach this lovely park by driving 25 miles east of 1-65 and 10 miles east of the Alabama Space & Rocket Center off of highway 431 or highway 72.

I have described the Hawk's View, Gum Tree Lane & White Oak trails together, since they originate as one trail and branch off into separate trails, before merging again. I also described the Mountain Mist Trail from its southern most point, since the northern portion of the trail "quietly" ends at a junction with an old road and no trail sign. The Warpath Ridge Scout Trail originates in the park and both parallels and merges with the Hawk's View Trail until O'Shaughnessy Point. Both trails have red trail markers-and numerous paths seem to join the two trails, thus confusing some hikers.

Trail maps are available at the park showing the locations of the trails.

GUM TREE LANE TRAIL/ WHITE OAK TRAIL/ HAWK'S VIEW TRAIL *Easy*

These three trails all originate at the same location and later branch in different directions. The trails start at the east end of the parking lot area near the park office. The "combination" trail gradually ascends in a SE direction and reaches the ridge at approximately 1 1/2 miles. Here, the trail crosses the road where the pavement ends. (the paved road leads past the rental cottages along the ridge and back to the parking area and park office) The gravel road leads S along the ridge.

The trail now follows the ridge S and passes a rest shelter and several views from rock cliffs before intersecting the gravel road mentioned earlier. For a shorter hike, bear right on the road, which leads back to the paved road. The White Oak Trail abruptly appears on your left and Leads W. Continue S along the gravel road, passing another rest shelter on your left and a rocky trail that descends to

Monte Sano State Park

intersect the Mountain Mist Trail. Just past this intersecting trail, the Gum Tree Lane Trail will bear right and lead W. Both the White Oak and Gum Tree Lane trails rejoin the Hawk's View Trail on the west side of the ridge.

Soon after the Gum Tree Lane trail junction, the gravel road swings right and ends at a fire tower. From this point on, the trail becomes the Hawk's View Trail. It continues S along the ridge, passing another rest shelter and a short distance later intersects the Mountain Mist Trail. (This trail descends briefly and leads N below the ridge) The trail soon reaches O'Shaughnessy Point and a junction with the Warpath Ridge Scout Trail. (This trail leads another 10 miles southeast) This location affords fine views to the south and west. From this point, the trail turns abruptly NW and follows the ridge back to the parking area. Pass another rest shelter on your left and soon thereafter a trail that descends from the ridge. This trail leads below the picnic area in the park before ascending Round Top Mountain. The trail thereafter is now incomplete due to building construction.

You can however ascend to the picnic area. Hawk's View Trail continues along the ridge, passing another rest shelter. A short distance later, the Gum Tree Lane Trail intersects and the White Oak Trail also intersects a short distance from that point. From that point, the "combination" trail continues NW and ends at the Parking lot. The Warpath Ridge Scout Trail parallels the Hawk's View Trail from O'Shaughnessy Point to where the Gum Tree Lane Trail intersects and then follows the edge of the ridge before ending at the Amphitheater area.

I found the west side of the ridge somewhat confusing with numerous paths "connecting" the Hawk's View and Warpath Ridge Scout Trails. You still wind up at or near the parking area however. These trails are easy to walk and make a very nice dayhike.

MOUNTAIN MIST TRAIL *Moderate*

This seemingly secluded trail begins a few hundred yards north of O'Shaughnessy Point on the Hawk's View Trail. From the trail sign, descend sharply by way of switchbacks before heading north below the ridge. This trail is narrow and very rocky. I recommend good hiking boots. The first two miles lead north, paralleling the ridge above. A short but rocky connector trail on your left ascends to the ridge at approximately 1 mile. Passing under several rock overhangs and cliff formations, the trail continues north. Several rest shelters and a number of rental cottages are located on the ridge above.

At approximately 2.0 miles another connector trail ascends to the ridge above after passing several of the cottages overlooking the trail. A short distance later, the trail makes a sharp turn to the right. (The remains of an old logging road will continue NW below the ridge, passing several more cottages before intersecting another old road. A short trail ascends to the paved road above just before this intersection of old logging roads) After a gradual descent, pass an old decaying rest shelter.

Here the trail swings back to the north and begins ascending to a small ridge. After passing the old shelter remains, an old logging road will lead NW approximately 2 miles and intersect the old road previously mentioned. This road leads west and will end at the paved road (Bankhead Parkway) leading back to the main park facilities.

Upon reaching the ridge, the trail splits. The main trail continues north along the ridge. The trail branching off to the right ascends to the ridge top before passing by, through and even under some very large rock formations appropriately called Stone Cuts. This short trail then rejoins the main trail. A short distance further, a spur trail leads R and ascends to Logan Point with views of the valley below. The main trail turns NW and gradually descends to intersect the logging road previously mentioned. This road leads west to the paved road leading back to the park facilities.

I have described this trail from its southern terminus. By hiking down the connector trail by the cottages, you can hike south to O'Shaughnessy Point and return via the Hawk's View Trail or hike just the northern part of the trail. A number of options allow the hiker to choose his own route. When in the Huntsville area, stop by this lovely state park and enjoy the hiking trails.

BLACK WALNUT TRAIL *Easy*

This trail begins across the paved road from the overlook just north of the park office. It passes by the Observatory and basically descends the entire way before ending at the same paved road (Bankhead Parkway). The campground will be on your left and the paved road on your right.

I found the other trails in the park more interesting, but this trail is convenient for those camping closeby.

RICKWOOD CAVERNS
STATE PARK

This unique state park does not have a lake or mountainous terrain as its main attraction, but rather a magnificent underground cave. Located just north of Birmingham, the park is centrally located and offers not only the cave, but also improved and primitive camping, a picnic area, swimming pool, miniature golf and two hiking trails.

The shorter of the two trails is an easy walk on a wide path, making a loop back to the parking area while the longer trail provides a more moderate hike with rocky terrain and some uphill and downhill sections.

Rickwood Caverns State Park can be reached by taking exit 284 off of 1-65 north of Warrior and following the signs.

SHORT TRAIL *Easy*

This easy to walk trail starts at the edge of the parking area. The wide trail is relatively flat and easy to follow. Walk E for approximately .3 mile and reach a junction. Walk to your left and follow the looping trail as it winds its way back to a southerly direction. The trail will turn W briefly and reach the junction mentioned earlier at approximately .7 mile.

FOSSIL MT. TRAIL *Moderate*

This trail is narrow and was quite overgrown when I attempted to hike it. From the carpet golf area, walk N, as the trail will make its way around the ridge area. Reach an intersection at approximately .4 mile. Here, I found the trail ahead poorly marked and overgrown. Bear left where the "connector" trail intersected the main trail and ascend. The connector trail will cross the ridge to the west side and bear S. Reach the starting point at approximately 1.3 miles.

The trail map and trail mileage did not agree when I walked this trail. Check with park personnel before hiking.

PRIVATE PROPERTY TRAILS

Along with national forest trails, state park trails and other government trails, a number of hiking trails are located on private property. Many of these trails are not publicized very much, if at all. Although some trails have been closed to the public, corporate and individual land owners have allowed scout groups and other outdoor clubs and groups to use the trails on their property. Some of these trails may require payment of a fee to the landowner. Others may require notification to the landowner of the group wishing to hike the trail. Respecting the rights of others and respecting the land by not "leaving trash behind" helps greatly to promote continued cooperation between landowners and future hikers.

The following trails lead the hiker through a variety of terrain and natural features, sometimes not found on public trails, such as Rock Bridge Canyon Nature Trail and the Dismals Nature trail.

HURRICANE CREEK PARK *Moderate*

This very interesting trail is situated on an 80 acre tract of land along Hurricane Creek north of Cullman. From the souvenir and ticket counter, you walk east along the ridge and past a small waterfall. Here, the trail splits. The Low Trail descends to your right into the canyon. The High Trail continues along the ridge. You will pass a natural rock bridge and overhanging rock before the trail descends to your right. Upon reaching the creek, you will bear to your right heading west along the creek. When you come to the picnic area with a covered pavilion, you will pass a small waterfall on your left.

From the picnic area, you can either take the Low Trail back to the entrance or cross the suspension bridge over Hurricane Creek. Another short trail will lead from the picnic pavilion along the creek to the cable car exit up to the entrance gate.

After crossing the suspension bridge, the main trail will bear left. The short cut to your right again offers a shorter hiking distance for those who may not wish to hike the longer trail. From the fork, bear left and soon reach Twilite Tunnel. An alternate trail bypasses the tunnel for those who do not like the dark and narrow pass through the rock.

After ascending from the tunnel, the main trail continues on your right. Ascend to the ridge above and head west above the creek. You will soon reach the "Bottle Neck", a narrow opening in the large boulder. Again, an alternate path allows those who cannot squeeze through the rock to continue on the trail.

Within a few hundred yards, the trail begins to descend by way of switchbacks. You will soon reach a sign, where the trail to your right leads back to the suspension bridge. Continue to descend and cross the creek by way of boards over the rocks. After crossing the creek, you will ascend and pass under a rock ledge before reaching the wooden cable car. For those who do not wish to ascend the steep trail, the large bell can be rung and the proprietor will bring you back to the starting platform by way of the small cable car.

The length of this trail is a little over two miles, unless you take the alternate short trails. The mountain laurel is very pretty in season and the hardwood trees make this a nice walk in the Fall. Mr. William E. Rodgers has operated it for over 28 years. The modest cost is well worth the effort to walk this interesting trail. The park can be reached by driving north of Cullman on U.S. Highway 31, approximately 6 miles north of the Hwy 31 /Hwy 157 junction.

DISMALS CANYON *Easy*

This unique canyon area was opened to the public in 1952 and has been declared a natural wilderness by the National Geographic Society. It has become famous for its dismalites, which glow in the dark. (night tours are given) The trail begins at the wooden platform at the end of the concrete sidewalk leading from the store and canoe rental building.

Wooden steps descend from the platform into the canyon. You immediately pass Rainbow Falls with a wooden bridge passing over the creek. You can walk either direction, since the first part of the trail makes a loop. If you walk right, the trail makes its way through the canyon, past a number of rock formations. You will feel the cool canyon breeze that makes this walk enjoyable, even in the hot summer months. The latter part of the trail also makes a loop back to the main trail. The total distance of the trail is approximately over 1 mile, but the terrain and many features make it seen a bit longer. The Canyon is presently being operated by Mr. Trent Stephenson, Route 3 Box 281, Phil Campbell, Al. 35581

The Dismals Canyon is located approximately 12 miles south of Russellville off of U.S. Highway 43 on County Road 8.

ROCK BRIDGE CANYON   *Moderate*

This unique canyon provides for a very interesting hike along canyan walls, beside waterfalls and natural springs and past huge chestnut oak trees.

The trail begins at the parking area where the entrance road ends. If you ascend to your left, you quickly come to wooden stairs. The one straight ahead leads up to an old indian cave shelter. The wooden stairs on your right ascend to and allow you to walk over a large stone natural bridge formation. This trail then ascends to a small wooden building on the entrance road. This was the original trail leading into the canyon.

If you take the trail to your right before climbing either set of wooden stairs, you will descend to a rock shelter. (wooden picnic tables allow you to rest and enjoy the view above of the natural stone bridge mentioned earlier) From here the trail makes its way along the canyon wall before passing through two large boulders with water flowing from a nearby spring.

After passing through the boulders, you can bear right and cross the small pond by way of an old wooden bridge. The main trail ascends to your left and continues along the canyon walls, passing huge chestnut oak trees. You will soon pass by a nice waterfall flowing from the canyon rim. (The wooden footbridge may not be usable due to flood damage, but you can carefully cross the rocks without getting wet)

From here, the trail will continue along the canyon wall before descending to yrour right and crossing an unnamed creek. Unusual rock formations and a vertical crack in one large wall, from which an underground spring can be heard, help make this canyon excursion worth the visit. After crossing the creek, the main trail bears right and soon reaches the parking area. A short side trail to your left leads downstream, where nice views of another waterfall can be seen.

The total distance of the trail may be a little over 1/2 mile, but the many attractions make it seem longer. The canyon and trail has been operated since 1957 by Mrs. Mary Avery, Route 1 Box 151, Hodges, Al. 35571.

The canyon is located just off Al. Highway 172 west of Hamilton on County Road 45.

NATURAL BRIDGE   *Easy*

This walking trail is named after the large sandstone arches formed thousands of years ago by water erosion. The wide path starts at the ticket and souvenir building. From the building, cross a wooden footbridge and follow the signs.

The trail basically follows below and under the large natural stone bridge and continues along the canyon walls. Along the trail, you will find a number of ferns, giant magnolias and mountain laurel.

At approximately 1/4 mile, come to the end of the canyon, where a small creek descends from right to left. Bear left, making a 180 degree turn and follow the wide gravel path. Cross several wooden footbridges over the small creek before reaching the entrance building.

Picnic facilities as well as camping sites make this a nice family outing or group excursion. Natural Bridge is located just off of U.S. Highway 278, west of the junction with Ala. State Highway 5. It is open all year round. For information you can call (205) 486-5330.

GOVERNMENT TRAILS

I have included in this section all trails located on government properties. These include federal, state, county and municipal trails.

Some trails are located on properties administered by the National Park Service. These include Horseshoe Bend National Military Park. Other trails are located on state properties, including trails in Tannehill Historical State Park near Birmingham. Still other trails are located on county and municipal land.

The U.S. Army Corps of Engineers maintains a number of recreational facilities with a number of hiking trails included. The Tennessee Valley Authority also maintains several trails in the Muscle Shoals area. I have only included one TVA trail and no U.S. Army Corps trails, since most of them are very short and sometimes paved, such as exercise or bike trails.

ROCKPILE TRAIL   *Moderate*

This TVA trail connects the Small Wild Area with Wilson Dam on the Tennessee River near Florence. From the parking area near the dam's visitor center, the trail will descend briefly from the trailhead sign via wooden steps before making its way along the bluff overlooking Pickwick Lake below Wilson Dam. At .3 mile, come to a sign at the edge of the picnic area. From here you will need to walk along the right side of the picnic area following the fence. You will reach a sign at the far end of the picnic area and soon descend via stairs.

At .7 mile, reach the paved road leading down to the public boat launch. Walk down this road, where a sign on your left notes the trail. From here, the trail briefly follows an old railroad bed before ascending.

At approximately 1.2 miles, descend to a gravel road leading down to a pump house facility. There is no sign located here, but the trail picks up again approximately 25 yards to your right after you cross the road and walk down the overgrown bank. (look for red paint on trees) The trail will ascend briefly and travel through thick forest area before descending to a service road at approximately 1.6 mile. Walk down this road approximately 100 yards and reach Pond Creek, a man made drainage ditch. At the time I hiked this trail, only two large telephone poles allowed passage across this sewage ditch.

UNTIL ANOTHER FOOTBRIDGE IS CONSTRUCTED, I DO NOT RECOMMEND TRYING TO CROSS THIS DRAINAGE DITCH.

After crossing the drainage ditch, the trail briefly ascends. It then wanders through thick forest and an overgrown area before passing under power lines and reaching another old road at approximately 2.2 miles. There is a fence across the road, but you can walk around it and see a sign 50' ahead. Turn left at the sign. This site was the location of the old Wilson Steam Plant (coal fired) built in 1918.

From the sign, the trail briefly descends on an old concrete sidewalk and crosses the concrete area. (A spur trail on the right leads down to the lake) The trail picks up on the other side of the concrete area. After passing through the fence built around the old site, the trail widens and soon reaches a parking area near the Small Wild Area at approximately 2.7 miles.

This moderate to strenuous trail offers a variety of terrain and good views of Wilson Dam. During summer months, some areas may be overgrown with briars and tall weeds. I recommend using a hiking stick. Also, be sure to carry plenty of water.

Wilson Dam is located just off U.S. Highway 43 south of Florence.

HISTORIC GORGE TRAIL *Moderate*

This rather unique trail is entirely located within the gorge area below the 100' falls of Noccalula Falls Park in Gadsden. After passing through the admission gate into the park, the entrance into the gorge area will be on your right. Walk down the steep staircase into the gorge and pick up the trail as it winds along the rocks toward the Falls. Make your way across the large rocks under the Falls. (Use caution, as the rocks are somewhat slippery from the moisture)

The remainder of the trail makes its way along the gorge, with

Historic Gorge Trail - Noccalula Falls

Black Creek on your left and cliff walls on your right. Markers are located along the trail and brochures for them are located at the entrance gate. After approximately 1 1/4 miles, the trail ends at a rock wall beside the creek. An old bridge that crossed the creek is no longer standing, thus forcing the hiker to retrace his steps back to stairs. Plans are to contruct a new bridge in the future.

Upon reaching the stairs, you can continue walking along the gorge for another .2 mile before ascending up to the plateau area above the gorge.

HORSESHOE BEND NATIONAL MILITARY PARK

This National Military Park is situated at the site of the famous 1814 battle against the Creek Indian Nation by General Andrew Jackson's Army. It is located 18 miles northeast of Alexander City and 12 miles north of Dadeville on Ala. Highway 49. There are two trails within the park. The 2.8 mile Nature Trail is located within the horseshoe shaped peninsula and the 2.0 mile Loop Trail is located across the highway near the outer boundary of the park. A third trail, The Horseshoe Bend Trail was a 10 mile BSA trail that linked Ala. Hwy 22 and HWY 49 near the park, but recent hunting permits on nearby private land have created a problem with trail location. (Inquiries at the park office can be made as to the feasibility of hiking this trail)

NATURE TRAIL *Easy*

This 2.8 mile trail begins at the parking area for the Overlook Hill just south of the visitor center. From here, it wanders south to Gun Hill before crossing the paved road.

The trail will cross the paved park road two more times as it changes direction, heading east towards the Tallapoosa River. Here, the trail swings north and parallels the river for a distance before ending back at Overlook Hill.

This is a nice walking trail through the battlefield area, especially in early Spring or late Fall.

LOOP TRAIL *Easy*

This 2.0 mile trail starts across Highway 49 from the entrance to the park. After walking through the fence, the trail heads West into the woods. At approximately 130 yards, where the trail veers right, look for the marked trees on your left. Take this route, which heads south along the ridge before descending to the Tallapoosa River. At approximately .4 mile , reach the river and turn right onto a fire road. You will soon cross a footbridge and continue walking west, parallel to the river. At approximately .9 mile, you will reach the park boundary.

Here, the trail will bear NE on the service road. This road will gradually ascend and eventually fork after approximately 1.5 miles. Take the right fork, which heads east and gradually veers south. At approximately 2.0 miles, the trail finishes its loop and ends at the fence where you started.

This trail has been changed from a 4 mile trail to its present 2 mile loop trail and signs were not posted at the time I hiked it. Please check at the visitor center before walking this trail. Unlike the nature trail, this trail is more remote and also more difficult to hike. Plan to take water and also let others know you are hiking this trail.

PALISADES PARK TRAILS *Easy*

This 90 acre park is located approximately 5 1/2 miles north of Oneanta off of U.S. Highway 231. It is operated by the Blount County Park & Recreation Board. Shelters, picnic tables & grills make this a great day use area.

There are approximately 4 miles of walking trails on top of and along the ridge of Ebell Mtn, with numerous overlooks. Information can be obtained by contacting the park at Route 3 Box 169, Oneonta, Al. 35121 or calling (205) 274-0017

Palisades Park

RUFFNER MOUNTAIN

This 538 acre forest and wildlife sanctuary lies within the city limits of Alabama's largest city. Here you will find a variety of plant and animal life along with a nature center offering education and recreational programs for the community.

There are a number of hiking trails on Ruffner Mountain, ranging from 1/4 mile to 5 miles. The two shortest trails are the Trillium Trail, which intersects the Quarry Trail near the paved road leading to the old fire tower on top of Ruffner Mountain and the Silent Journey Trail which departs and rejoins the Quarry Trail as it winds along the ridge toward the rock quarry.

The Geology Trail is a 1/2 mile trail leading from the nature center to its junction with the Marian Harnach Nature Trail. The Marian Harnach Nature Trail is a 1 mile loop trail that starts and ends at the Nature Center. These two trails are short enough for the children to walk and enjoy the surrounding hardwood forest.

The Quarry Trail is a 1 1/2 miles trail leading to an old rock quarry. The 5 Mile Trail is actually a 2 mile loop trail that departs the Quarry Trail and rejoins it after circling the rock quarry. The return hike back to the Nature Center makes the length of the hike 5 miles. (3 miles round trip for the Quarry Trail) I have described the Quarry Trail and 5 Mile Trail since these trails are longer and require sufficient time to walk.

QUARRY TRAIL *Easy*

This trail departs from the Geology trail near the nature center. It gradually ascends west to the ridge of Ruffner Mountain. At approximately .2 mile, cross the paved road, which leads to the old fire tower atop Ruffner Mountain. (the Trillium Trail descends to your right) Continue ascending and reach the ridge at approximately .5 mile. (the old trail ascends to your left) Continue hiking along the ridge before intersecting the Silent Journey Trail at approximately 1 mile. (this trail descends and rejoins the Quarry Trail after a short 1/4 mile walk) At approximately 1.2 miles the trail will descend to your left and make its way around the ridge.

At approximately 1.5 mile, reach an overlook above the quarry with views of the city beyond. The trail continues for a short distance before arriving at the rock quarry.

Those not electing to continue on the 5 Mile Trail have a 1 1/2 miles return hike back to the Nature Center and parking area.

5 MILE TRAIL *Moderate*

This trail is really misnamed, since it only makes a 2 mile loop around the rock quarry and rejoins the Quarry Trail. From the Nature Center however, the complete round trip hike does encompass about 5 miles. (including the Quarry Trail)

From the Overlook of the quarry, bear left at the fork. The trail begins to descend shortly after leaving the top of the ridge. I passed two trail signs when I hiked this trail. Both had been pulled out of the ground by vandals. After a short ascent, reach a junction with a trail on your right, which leads back to the Overlook above the quarry.

At approximately .5 mile, just past the junction mentioned, the trail descends and makes a turn back to the right. At approximately .8 mile, reach an overgrown area of kudzu. The trail will continue on your right. After walking through the overgrown area- you will continue on an old service road. The remainder of this trail follows this wide path around the quarry. Two short spur trails on your right lead to the quarry on the other side of the small ridge. At approximately 2.0 miles, you will come to the junction with the Quarry Trail. Continue on the Quarry Trail back to the Nature Center.

I would suggest that anyone hiking the Quarry and 5 Mile trails carry water and snack foods. Be sure to obtain maps and information from the Nature Center personnel before hiking these trails for the first time.

TANNEHILL HISTORICAL STATE PARK

Created in 1969, this 1500 acre park lies in the corners of Jefferson, Tuscaloosa and Bibb Counties. Located within 30 minutes from downtown Birmingham, this park is considered the birthplace of the Birmingham iron industry.

The first forge was built in 1830 by Daniel Hillman. A charcoal blast furnace was added in 1855, with two more furnaces added in 1863. During the Civil War, these furnaces produced 20 tons of pig iron a day for the Confederacy. On March 31st in 1865, the facility was destroyed by the Union Army.

Extensive restoration, with over 40 structures, has the Tannehill Ironworks listed on the National Register of Historic Places.

With 168 improved campsite, 50 additional tent sites and over 8 miles of trails, the park is a great place to bring the family. On the third weekend of each month, many folks come to Tannehill for the Trade Days, a large "flea market" with selling and trading of just about anything.

Since most of the trails are short distances, I have only described the Slave Quarters Trail and the Iron Road. The 18 mile Bucksville to Montevallo Stage Road built in 1815 can be hiked by Boy Scout Organization with permission from park personnel, since much of the route lies on private property.

The park can be reached by taking exit 100 (Bucksville) off of 1-59 west of Birmingham or exit 1 (McCalla) off of 1-459.

IRON ROAD   *Easy*

This trail is listed in the park brochure as being 2.5 miles in length, but I found it to be closer to 1.5 miles. The trail begins across Roupes Creek near the ironworks, at a junction with the Slave Quarters Trail.

From the junction, the trail gradually ascends for the first .3 mile. Roupes Creek will be on your right. After a brief descent, the trail continues along the creek. Another short ascent up a second ridge and the trail will level out for awhile. At approximately .7 mile, reach an old roadbed before descending briefly. For the next .5 mile the trail is somewhat level before ascending a third ridge at approximately 1.2 miles.

Near its junction with the 1815 Bucksville to Montevallo Stage Road, a sign on your right marks a short trail leading left to an old slave cemetery. Here are several hundred graves where slaves, who worked at the ironworks, were buried. At approximately 1.6 miles. the trail will intersect the Bucksville to Montevallo Stage Road. This old road is restricted to Scout Organizations who wish to hike the 18 miles, since most of the roadbed lies on private property. By bearing left on this road, you could hike back to the main park property and complete a loop hike by taking the Slave Quarters Trail to where you started your hike on the Iron Road.

SLAVE QUARTERS TRAIL   *Easy*

This 1.7 mile trail begins across the wooden bridge near the visitor information center. After crossing the bridge over Roupes Creek, bear right along the creek. After a short distance, you will cross a small footbridge and reach a trail junction.

The Iron Road Trail continues straight ahead. To your right is a bridge crossing Roupes Creek and the Tannehill Furnaces. The Slave Quarters Trail will bear left and makes its way between two ridges, leading northeast. The trail is named for the houses where the slaves, who worked the furnaces, lived.

At approximately 1.7 miles, the trail intersects the Bucksville to Montevallo Stage Road. (This old road is restricted to Boy Scout groups who wish to backpack the 18 miles trail leading to Montevallo) Those who do not wish to hike back an the same trail may elect to bear right on the Bucksville to Montevallo Road until it junctions with the Iron Road Trail, and hike that trail back to the trailhead. They may also bear left and walk back to the main park area, where on the third weekend of each month, Trade Days are held.

Lookout Mountain Trail

102.

LOOKOUT MOUNTAIN TRAIL

This unique "collection" of trails has grown to become Alabama's second longest trail. (only the Pinhoti Trail is longer) Doyal Benefield, Desoto State Park manager during the 1970's, is credited for conceiving the idea for the Lookout Mountain Trail. In 1968, 7 miles of trails along Little River inside Little River Canyon were completed. In 1973, the Desoto Scout Trail stretched 16 miles from the Comer Scout Reservation north of the park to the Edna Hill Church south of the park. In 1986, 9 miles of trail opened along Lookout Mountain between Cherokee Rock Village and Gadsden.

Today, the trail stretches some 72 miles from Gadsden to Mentone, Al. Efforts to merge with the Bluff Trail near Chattanooga and Cloudland State Park in Georgia to form a 125 mile long trail have not materialized.

This trail is unique in that it includes the mountain ridge, an abandoned railroad bed, 29 miles of paved road and the section along the Little River, the only river that begins and ends on top of a mountain. (plateau) I have divided the trail into 5 sections, with two sections being along paved roads.

At present, the only parking areas available for vehicles are located at Desoto State Park, Cherokee Rock Village and at Little River Canyon Mouth Campground. Hikers on the southern part of the trail may encounter horseback riders, ATV's and mountain bikers, since a number of roads cross the mountain and allow access to the trail.

Drinking water is very limited along the trail. Sandrock House Springs is probably the only reliable source along the 16 mile ridge from Gadsden to Cherokee Rock Village. The fishcamp store near Yellow Creek Falls and Little River Canyon Mouth Campground are sources along the middle section of the trail. Desoto State Park and the town of Mentone have water available on the northern section of the trail.

Maps of the trail can be obtained by writing to: LOOKOUT MOUNTAIN TRAIL, c/o Danny Crownover, 615 Bellevue Drive, Gadsden Al. 35901.

Lookout Mountain Trail - Yellow Creek Falls

104.

I have chosen to begin hiking from Overlook Drive in Gadsden due to the first section of trail below Paseur Park Overlook being extremely overgrown and the presence of considerable broken glass along the trail. One other area south of Desoto State Park was also completely overgrown when I hiked it.

Until that area is cleared, I suggest hiking the Desoto Scout Trail along the Little River, from where the two trails split, to Desoto State Park.

Those hikers interested in hiking this trail should send inquiries to the address above for up-to-date information and maps.

SECTION 1 (18 Miles) *Moderate*
Paseur Park Overlook to Cherokee Rock Village

The first 2.0 miles of the trail were extremely overgrown and numerous broken glass bottles need to be cleared before the two mile area from Paseur Park Overlook to the paved road can be hiked. easily. I am therefore starting the trail description from Overlook Drive.

From the trail sign near the apartment building on your right, the trail will parallel the road briefly before continuing along the side of the ridge. At 2.2 miles, reach an old overgrown fire road. Continue along the ridge and pass under power lines at approximately 3.3 miles. Reach the Owl Hollow Trail at 3.8 miles. Ascend, steeply, to your left and at 4.0 miles, on the left, is the short Satellite Trail leading along the ridge to the radio tower and an overlook of the Shinbone Ridge area and Coosa River Valley. Belmont Drive, leading from Lay Springs Road to the tower, is one of several roads leading up to or over the mountain ridge. Continue until you reach the top at 4.2 miles.

From the trail junction, the Lookout Mountain Trail will continue along the top of the ridge. At approximately 5.3 miles, reach an overlook (Ken's Overlook) on your left with good views to the west. Descend briefly and continue along the ridge. Reach a gravel road at 5.8 miles leading to a microwave tower. Walk along the gravel road to the tower. The trail will bear to your right and pass around the fence. Descend briefly and cross Glen Gap Road at 6.0 miles. (this road crosses over the ridge from Lay Springs Road, through Daisy Gap, to Owl Hollow Road on the E side of the ridge)

Ascend after crossing the road. The trail continues along the ridge, making several ascents and descents. Reach a dirt jeep road on your left at approximately 8.1 miles. This road descends to the Lake Louise Road and Lay Springs Road. (this road is known as the Sand Pit Trail) Continue along the ridge.

In a few minutes, it will go down a steep descent. Reach an overlook on your right at 8.5 miles. This is a nice place to camp. Continue along the ridge before ascending steeply at 9.0 miles. and leveling out again. The trail will descend again. Reach another trail on your left at approximately 9.8 miles. This is the Chicken House Trail, which also descends to Lay Springs Road.

A second trail on your left descends approximately 300' to a reliable spring,. Ascend steeply for a short distance, where a third trail leads to your left. This trail leads 300' to Sandrock House Overlook, with views to the west. This is also a good camping area. At mileage 10.0, this location is approximately half way between Overlook Drive in Gadsden and Cherokee Rock Village.

Walk back to the trail and continue along the ridge. You will ascend briefly and reach the Powerline Overlook on your right, with good views to the east. The trail will soon descend, level out, ascend and level out again. Pass by an old road on your left at 11.4 miles. The trail will ascend again, level out and ascend. Reach a rocky area with a small campsite on your right at 11.9 miles. The trail will soon split. Take the right fork. You will soon reach Doyal's Overlook, with great views of Shinbone Ridge, the Coosa River and the Piedmont area to the east at 12.4 miles.

Cross a rocky area. The trail will continue on your left. Reach Big Mountain Overlook at 12.9 miles. After 300', bear left on the dirt road, which leads back to the main trail. At approximately 13.9 miles, reach Bigfoot Trail, a side trail descending down to a public road on the east side of the ridge. The trail will then ascend and level out. Reach Jack's Jumpoff at approximately 15.4 miles, with great views of Weiss Lake, the Talledega Mountains and the Coosa valley.

Continue along the ridge, making a long descent before leveling out. At 15.9 miles, reach a wide logging road to your left. This is Lay Springs Trail, which descends to Lay Springs Road. Ascend along the dirt road and reach the Huff Gap Trail at approximately 16.3 miles. This trail descends to the old T.A.G. railroad. A trail sign marks the junction of Huff Gap Trail with the Lookout Mountain Trail.

Continue ascending on the dirt road and bear left after reaching the top of the ridge. The road will level out and also get narrow again. Reach Peach Orchard Shelter at 17.5 miles. This shelter is beyond repair. An old well nearby is also in very bad shape and cannot be used. The Crownover Loop Trail will split off to your left and rejoin the trail later. Continue straight ahead and reach Cherokee Rock Village at 18.0 miles. This area offers great views of Weiss Lake below.

Paseur Park Overlook is located near Noccalula Falls in Gadsden and north of the Ala. 227-U.S.431/278 junction, just off Harts Avenue. Cherokee Rock Village can be reached by taking the Lookout Mountain Parkway north from Noccalula Falls for 16.4 miles. Turn right (E) onto County Road 36 and travel 3.4 miles. Turn right onto an unmarked road and travel .6 mile before making a sharp curve to the right. The gravel road continues another 2.7 miles up to Cherokee Rock Village. This location is very popular with rock climbers as well as those who take in the great views of Weiss Lake and the Coosa valley from atop the huge rock formations.

SECTION 2 (13.1 Miles) *Moderate*
Cherokee Rock Village to Little River Canyon
Mouth Campground

The first 2.7 miles is a walk down the gravel road that leads up to Cherokee Rock Village. After passing under the power lines, the main road will turn left and continue .6 miles to County Road 36. Straight ahead is a dead end. The trail will turn to your right and descend .7 mile on an old dirt road before reaching the old T.A.G. (Tennessee, Alabama, Georgia) railroad bed. Turn left (N) on the

107.

Lookout Mountain Trail -
Old Tennessee, Alabama, Georgia (TAG) Railroad Bed

108.

tracks and continue along the abandoned roadbed. Cross under the Ala. Hwy 68 bridge at 3.8 miles.

At 4.1 miles, pass by an old grain mill and cross the gravel road just ahead. Continue along the tracks for the next 2.8 miles. This section of trail is not very scenic except for Yellow Creek Falls ahead. Reach the old T.A.G. Railroad bridge over Weiss Lake at approximately 6.9 miles. A spur trail to your left will lead to Yellow Creek Falls, a beautiful waterfall dropping off the mountain into Weiss Lake.

Since the old bridge has been removed, you will have to walk to your right down a dirt road to Ala. Hwy 273, cross the bridge, and walk up another gravel road to the railroad tracks on the other side of the lake.

From the northern end of the bridge, the trail continues along the roadbed. Cross County Road 48 at approximately 8.6 miles. Continue along the roadbed. Reach another paved road at 9.6 miles. Turn left and walk along the road for .4 miles, crossing two small creeks. The trail will continue on your right after crossing the 2nd bridge. (the old railroad bridges are practically destroyed from flooding) Continue along the railroad bed for another 2 1/2 miles.

Reach the paved road leading to the Little River Canyon Mouth Campground and the Rim Drive above the canyon. Walk down this road to your left for .6 miles and reach the campground at 13.1 miles. Little River Canyon Mouth Campground is located at the mouth of Little River Canyon, the deepest canyon east of the Rocky Mountains. It has developed and primitive campsites, along with a picnic area and playground. After a long day of hiking, the campground offers a nice place to camp.

The campground & park can be reached by way of the Canyon Rim Drive or Ala. Hwy 273 south of Ala. Hwy 35. Cherokee Rock Village can be reached by turning onto County Road 36, 16.4 miles north of Gadsden, and driving east for 3.4 miles. Turn south onto an unmarked road. This road takes a sharp curve to the right after .6 mile and continues uphill for another 2.7 miles to Cherokee Rock Village. This site offers fantastic views of Weiss Lake and the Coosa valley from atop the huge boulders. Rock climbing is very

Lookout Mountain Trail - Little River Canyon

110.

popular here also.

SECTION 3 (21 Miles)   *Moderate*
Little River Canyon Mouth Campground to Ala. Hwy 35

This section or the trail follows the west rim of Little River Canyon for the next 21 miles. The paved road ascends from the campground entrance to the western rim of the canyon and follows the canyon northward.

Attractions to be seen along this Rim Parkway include Eberhart Point Park, with great views northward into Little River Canyon, Crow's Point, with great views southward into the canyon, Grace's High Falls on the south edge of Bear Creek and Umbrella Rock, a unique rock formation in the middle of the road. Little River Falls, a 60' waterfall is located just south of Ala. Hwy 35. This is the beginning of the canyon.

Section 4 continues north of highway 35 near the Edna Hill Church. For those, who may wish to travel the Rim Drive, the 21 mile roadway may be reached by taking Ala. Hwy 35 east from Ft. Payne & I-59 or Ala. Hwy 68 east from Collinsville and turning north on Ala. Hwy 273 for 9 miles.

SECTION 4 (12.5 Miles)   *Moderate*
Edna Hill Church to Desoto State Park (West Entrance)

This section of the trail picks up again north of Alabama Hwy 35. From the bridge over Little River, drive 1 mile west towards Ft. Payne. Turn right (N) onto a gravel road and go .8 mile to the Edna Hill Church, the southern terminus of the Desoto Scout Trail (D.S.T.). This church was organized in 1907 and served by "Circuit Riders". There is plenty of room for parking next to the old church.

From the church, walk down the road .2 mile. After the road turns left, take the 2nd road on your right. (straight ahead is private property) Cross a small creek after 200 yards and notice a DST sign on your right. You will notice DST signs along the jeep road at various distances. At approximately 1.0 mile, you will pass a DST Mile #13 sign on your left. Bear to your right (E) at 1.8 miles, where a road on your left intersects the trail. A "food plot" area lies to the left after the two roads intersect. Descend and cross Hurricane Creek at approximately 2.0 miles. Continue on the roadbed.

At approximately 2.6 miles, two roads will intersect the trail, one on your left and one on your right. (The road to the right leads a short distance to Billy's Ford, an area where fording the river allowed early settlers access to the wilderness region) Notice another DST sign on your right at approximately 3.1 miles, where the trail will descend. Cross a small creek, where a side road ascends on your left. The trail will ascend for a short distance. Bear right (E) on top of the ridge.

At approximately 3.8 miles, reach the Little River at Hartline Ford, another area that allowed settlers to cross the river. The trail will cross over a small creek here & continue N parallel to the river. At 4.0 miles, notice a road on your left. Ascend N for a short distance at 4.3 miles. You will pass by another "food plot" on your left. Cross a small creek at approximately 4.9 miles. Pass by several DST signs. At approximately 5.3 miles, cross a small creek. The Desoto Scout Trail (DST) will bear right (E) towards the Little River and a campsite used by scouting groups and other hikers. The trail will ascend after crossing the creek and bear left (NW). Reach the top of the ridge at approximately 5.7 miles and continue NW. Pass by "food plot" areas on each side of the road at approximately 6.1 miles. Ascend for 200 yards, where a side trail on your right will lead E. The main trail will bear left, continuing NW, with a side road on your left that leads SW. (Just before another food plot on your left).

At approximately 6.7 miles, some 300 yards past the food plot, the trail will leave the jeep road and take an abrupt right turn. Come to a fenced area just off the road. Continue along the fence on your right until you reach the corner of the field. Here, cross onto the right side of the fence. This area was extremely overgrown when I hiked it and nearly impassable. Until this area is cleared and marked, I strongly recommend hiking the DST trail along the Little River to Desoto State Park.

At approximately 8.0 miles, the trail will reach Straight Creek near an old stone CCC bridge. Pass under the bridge ruins and cross the creek by way of the rocks in the creekbed. Ascend to the park service road on the far side of the creek. Hike along this road for the next 1.9 miles. (At approximately 9.0 miles, a side trail on your right descends down to the Little River and DST Trail) Continue on the service roadbed. The trail will bear right (N) 100 yards before the end of the service road and chained entrance.

The next 1.5 miles of the trail, known as the Deep Woods Trail within Desoto State Park, will parallel Little River and the DST Trail. After passing by the picnic area, swimming pool and tennis courts, the trail will bear left and cross County Road 89 near the rock bridge church and north entrance to the park. From here, it will continue another 1.5 miles NW before reaching the Desoto Parkway near the west entrance to the park. For a more detailed notation off the trail, refer to the Deep Woods Trail in the Desoto State Park chapter.

Section 5 of the trail covers the distance from the park to Mentone.

SECTION 5 (8.3 Miles) *Easy*
Desoto State Park to Mentone

This last section of the trail is also along paved road. From the western entrance to Desoto State Park, the trail merges with the Desoto Parkway. The trail and road then merge with the Lookout Mountain Scenic Parkway. At Tutwiler Gap, the Desoto Parkway descends to merge with Ala. Hwy 117 at Valley Head. The Lookout Mountain Scenic Parkway & trail continue northward to Mentone. After passing through the junction with Ala Hwy 117 in Mentone, the Lookout Mountain Trail will end at the Eagle Nest Overlook at the park. This last overlook affords great views to the W.

The goal of extending the trail into Georgia and on to Chattanooga has yet to be realized. But maybe future endeavors could bring about such a great trail network.

Desoto State Park can be reached by taking Ala. Hwy 35 east from Ft. Payne and County Road 89 north for 5 miles. Mentone is north of the park on the same road.

SOURCES FOR ADDITIONAL INFORMATION

SIERRA CLUB/CAHABA GROUP
P.O. BOX 55591
BIRMINGHAM, AL. 35255

APPALACHIAN TRAIL CLUB OF ALABAMA
c/o Steve Hunt
909 LANDALE ROAD
BIRMINGHAM, AL. 35222

VULCAN TRAIL ASSOCIATION
P.O. BOX 19116
BIRMINGHAM, AL. 35219-9116

ALABAMA TRAILS ASSOCIATION
P.O. BOX 610311
BIRMINGHAM, AL. 35261-0311

LOOKOUT MOUNTAIN TRAIL ASSOCIATION
P.O. BOX 1434
GADSDEN, AL.35902

LOOKOUT MOUNTAIN TRAIL (Trail only)
615 BELLEVUE DRIVE
LOOKOUT MOUNTAIN
GADSDEN, AL. 35901-1601

ANNISTON OUTDOOR ASSOCIATION
C/O CITY OF ANNISTON
P.O. BOX 670
ANNISTON, AL. 36202

FOREST SUPERVISOR NATIONAL FORESTS IN ALABAMA
1765 HIGHLAND AVENUE
MONTGOMERY, AL 36107
(205) 832-4470

DISTRICT RANGER
USDA FOREST SERVICE
1001 NORTH STREET
(HIGHWAY 21 NORTH)
TALLADEGA, AL 35160
(205) 362-2909

DISTRICT RANGER
USDA FOREST SERVICE
450 HIGHWAY 46
HEFLIN, Al 362
(205) 463-2272

DISTRICT RANGER
USDA FOREST SERVICE
P.O. BOX 278
SOUTH MAIN STREET
DOUBLE SPRINGS, AL 35553

**ALABAMA DEPT. OF
CONSERVATION &
NATURAL RESOURCES**
DIVISION OF STATE
PARKS
64 NORTH UNION
STREET
MONTGOMERY, AL
36130
1-800-ALA-PARK
(Alabama only)
(205) 261-3333
(out-of-state)

**THE BANKHEAD
MONITOR , INC.**
P.O. BOX 117
MOULTON, AL 35650

CHEAHA STATE PARK
ROUTE 1, BOX 77-H
DELTA, AL 36258
(205) 488-5111

DESOTO STATE PARK
ROUTE 1, BOX 210
FORT PAYNE, AL 35967
(205) 845-5075

**JOE WHEELER
STATE PARK**
P.O. DRAWER K
ROGERSVILLE, AL 35652
1-800-544-JOEW (Resort)
(205) 247-1184
(Campground)

**LAKE GUNTERSVILLE
STATE PARK**
STAR ROUTE 63, BOX 224
GUNTERSVILLE, AL
35976-9126
(205) 582-2061 (Resort Inn)
(205) 582-8418
(Campground)

**LAKE LURLEEN
STATE PARK**
ROUTE 1, BOX 479
COKER, AL 35452
(205) 339-1558

**OAK MOUNTAIN
STATE PARK**
P.O. BOX 278
PELHAM, AL 35124
(205) 663-6783

**WIND CREEK
STATE PARK**
ROUTE 2, BOX 145
ALEXANDER CITY, AL
35010
(205) 329-0845

**BUCK'S POCKET
STATE PARK**
ROUTE 1, BOX 36
GROVEOAK, AL 35975
(205) 659-2000

**MONTE SANO
STATE PARK**
5101 NOLEN AVENUE
HUNTSVILLE, AL 35801
(205) 534-3757

**RICKWOOD CAVERNS
STATE PARK**
ROUTE 3, BOX 340
WARRIOR, AL 35180
(205) 647-9692

- NOTES -

- NOTES -

- NOTES -

- NOTES -

- NOTES -